WHAT I BELIEVE
AND WHY—
MAYBE

WHAT I BELIEVE
AND WHY—
MAYBE

Essays for the Modern World

by HORACE M. KALLEN

Edited by ALFRED J. MARROW

HORIZON PRESS   NEW YORK

Copyright © 1971 by Horace M. Kallen
Library of Congress Catalog Card No. 78-151012
ISBN 0-8180-1312-5
Manufactured in the United States of America

Foreword

Horace M. Kallen has been and is a very tough-minded man. He also has been and is a kind man, a generous man, a saintly man—a truly "good" man.

How is it possible to be a tough-minded man and a "good" man in a world that prefers non-rational or irrational myths to hard truths and seems to destroy those who do not live by guile and deception? These essays will show the reader how one Horace M. Kallen is able to do it.

Kallen has been a philosopher ever since his student days at Harvard. But a very special kind of philosopher—a lover of truth, a doubter of opinions, a defender of freedom, a believer in the communicating power of language, a hater of disguise and deceit, a promoter of reason and a protector of fairness and equal liberty. On this very partisan base, Kallen worked on eternal as well as topical problems in technical philosophy and he taught generations of Americans that they did not have to lose the values of their various heritages as they became a part of the American dream and as they accepted the American idea. The true American Dream of James Truslow Adams and the true American Idea of Theodore Parker.

This volume of collected essays does not address itself to displaying Kallen as a technical philosopher. Rather, this collection shows Kallen's widely ranging intellect dealing with everything from higher education to pacifism to psychology to God. No matter what the subject, Kallen's approach, analysis and conclusions are invariably informed by the scientific humanism which he began to absorb as a student of William James.

Horace M. Kallen has participated in the development of what some see as the first truly American philosophical attitude—radical empiricism. This movement got its real start when William James declared that psychology should be a natural science and that the then currently held view contrasting natural and moral sciences be abolished. Kallen, along with Peirce, F.C.S. Schiller, Dewey and others, fashioned the tools of pragmatic intelligence from this Jamesian beginning. These tools, contradictory and contested though they are, have made it possible for Americans to understand themselves better and progress as a unified nation.

In times such as these when many seem to be unsure of their intellectual moorings, we should re-read these formulators of American philosophy. They continually point toward new directions and ways of achieving a humane and just future.

These Kallen essays are a good start for a beginner; and a good refresher for those who may have forgotten.

JOHN R. EVERETT
President, The New School
for Social Research

Contents

Introduction

I first met Horace Kallen in my apartment in Greenwich Village in the mid-1930's. Though he was a star of the first magnitude in the American philosophical constellation (to borrow Sidney Hook's phrase), he did not hesitate to call at my home. He came, most generously, to offer his aid to Kurt Lewin, a refugee psychologist recently arrived from Nazi Germany, who was a house guest.

I quickly sensed that one cannot meet Kallen without experiencing a certain excitement: the power of his presence contrasts dramatically with his soft voice, gracious manner, and pervasive gentleness. It is not an excitement that fades on repeated exposure.

Little has changed since then in the way Kallen patterns his life. He continues to exemplify in his daily activities the most vital of all traditions in philosophy—philosophy not only as a way of life in a perplexing world, but as a rational activity. It takes as its point of departure the basic problems of human experience, and it

9

returns to them with imagination, insight, and understanding that help in their resolution.

In June 1970, Horace Kallen—then 87—completed more than fifty years of teaching at The New School, an association begun when the school was founded. Before that, he had taught philosophy and psychology at the University of Wisconsin, at Princeton, Harvard, and at Clark.

At Harvard, American philosophy was then in its golden age. William James, Josiah Royce, and George Santayana were at their best. Kallen became a favorite student and assistant of William James (who left his unfinished work, *Some Problems in Philosophy*, for Kallen to edit). He assisted George Santayana, who bequeathed his doctoral cap and gown to Kallen (he still dons them on occasions) and Josiah Royce. Barrett Wendell, professor of English, became one of Kallen's dear friends.

At The New School, where he taught from its founding in 1919 to his retirement in 1970, he was a close associate of Alvin Johnson, Thorstein Veblen, and James Harvey Robinson. Louis D. Brandeis, Benjamin Cardozo, and Edmond Cahn were among his friends. Although "emeritus," Kallen returns regularly to his office at The New School to meet with students and colleagues.

His workload remains heavy. He has written nearly forty books and more than 400 articles, all the while teaching and taking part in public affairs. No philosopher of our time has written as many books in as many diverse fields. His writings are insistently expressive of the pragmatist-humanist tradition. His special interest has been in extending pragmatic philosophy to the arts, education, culture, and religion. On each of these he has written significant books. Yet, he is a scholar with no appetite for the cloister. His life has been proof that one can be both a philosopher and a man of action, and gain from each role. His attitude toward himself and his work remains what it was when he wrote this self-portrait many years ago:

> Although I feel philosophy as a calling and enjoy teaching it, I have not been able to devote myself exclusively to what is euphemistically known as "scholarship" and the sheer academic life. My earliest interests were as literary as philosophical and were soon crossed by direct participation in political and economic move-

ments of the land, especially those aiming at the protection and growth of freedom. Hence, I have never attained that fullness of pedagogical withdrawal which custom and prejudice ordain for the practice of philosophy in America.

Unable to separate my profession from my life, I have always found myself ill at ease with the philosophy and the psychology of the schools. The first has seemed to me for the most part a ceremonial liturgy of professionals as artificial and detached from the realities of the daily life as bridge or chess or any other safe but exciting game of chance, and much of the second has seemed to me the sedulous elaboration of disregard for the living man of flesh and blood.

Kallen has confessed that his first and most enduring interest has been the development of aesthetic pragmatism. Yet the needs of society and the struggle for freedom have led him into many fields: "cooperative individualism," "cultural pluralism," "radical empiricism," "scientific humanism." In many ways he is the true embodiment of American philosophy, for his writings are notable expressions of his personal and unique concept of the philosophy of freedom. "The important thing," he once wrote, "becomes the mind's freedom to choose which to take from any and all ideas and events."

If the advancement of freedom has been one central theme, another has been "cultural pluralism"—the recognition of the diversity, the integrity, and what he calls the self-orchestration of mankind's cultures. The unity of mankind is this orchestration. Basic to it is the equal right of the different. Kallen holds that only out of the multiplicity of racial, ethnic, and religious characteristics does our creativity flow. And so he has plunged deeply into the practical problems in the mainstream of American life— civil liberties, education, religion, minority rights, unionism, Zionism, the cooperative movement. It is this that has made him, though born in Germany, the most American of philosophers living today. He keeps saying that he was made in Germany and improved in America.

Kallen's life and work, Hans Jonas has written, stands out as an example of "philosophical insight leading without a break to public commitment; theoretical conviction blending into social practice; a profound concern with education as non-separable from the pursuit of knowledge; and a humorous realism which, far from lessening the seriousness of the idea, makes it translatable into the give-and-take of human affairs and thus ensures the viability of an idealism that is at once effectual and non-tyrannical."

Raised in Boston in an orthodox Jewish home, intellectually nurtured at Harvard, Oxford, and Paris, Kallen has been a lifelong civil libertarian. He is wary of schools and movements and all improved uniformity. He has called the common urge to unify and amalgamate all differences a "primeval digestive passion" which, like the physical digestive system, works to convert all inputs into "homogenized 'unities.' " He understands that passion, but his own passion is for "the cooperation and teamwork of the different on equal terms." He prefers "correctness to consistency, truth to logic." He believes that unity cannot be achieved by coercion but only by voluntary cooperation.

In these days when groups seem to be at one another's throats, when advocates for this segment or that, of crusaders for liberation, minorities, conservatives, and revolutionaries all seem to be struggling to get at one another, is there any hope for voluntary cooperation? Horace Kallen says there is. By his life and his works, he shows us that hope and confidence can be as tough-minded as despair.

It is not tragedy that he holds to be the highest form of art, but rather comedy. Kallen sees tragedy as man's submission to despair and death, comedy as man's declaration of independence, his affirmation of faith in human triumph.

One cannot choose the "best" essays out of the body of Kallen's work. I have, therefore, tried in this collection to cover some of the major themes of Kallen's career as philosopher, educator, and advocate of equality in freedom. Hopefully, they will encourage readers to probe more deeply into the mind of this great American philosopher who has lighted the way for many in our time.

1 | What I Believe,
and Why—Maybe

It has been suggested that I might discuss "the ways in which a philosopher like yourself views political and moral problems and the philosophical grounds on which private action is based."

The invitation seemed to me a challenge to personal confession, to stand up and profess my philosophic faith and why I hold it. It was a challenge I felt I could not meet yet could not refuse. Accepting it, I wished I were a Sea Bee and could believe with their kind: "The difficult we do today; the impossible takes a little longer." But what most filled my mind was Shakespeare's words in *Much Ado about Nothing:* "For there was never yet philosopher who could endure the toothache patiently, however they have writ the style of the gods and made a push at chance and sufferance." And if this be the philosophers' way with the toothache, what could be their way with the headaches of "political and moral problems"?

So here I am, with a headache I couldn't refuse to suffer.

13

I do not recall that my philosophic vocation has enabled me to improve on a politician's or on that of any other trained specialist, such, say, as a dentist, regardless of the contrary faith of Plato and others of his ilk. In a vocation, happiness comes, as that recalcitrant pupil of Plato's, Aristotle declares, from "the exercise of vital powers along lines of excellence in a life affording them scope"—and is not such exercise the peculiar good that his vocation can produce for anyone's life? If the vocation of philosopher can do anything at all for the expert in any other vocation, say the political or societal expert, it might be to help the latter to set his own doings and sufferings in wider contexts of chance and sufferance. A philosopher *could* supplement and translate, even transvalue other specialties with his own. Presumably he could do this because his specialty is the universe and human-nature-in-the-universe.

As it happens, this is a specialty that other specialists have little use for, or none, even though each of them seems willy-nilly to develop more than a few traits of this philosophic form of exercising the vital powers. This form is a piecemeal dividing of answers to three broad questions. Briefly put, they are: 1. *What is it? 2. What is it for? What good, what use is it? How does it achieve what it's for? 3. How do you know?*

The answers to these questions constitute a world-picture, and philosophy is the art of creating world-pictures. However such pictures vary, their vital centre is a personal history—an individual and singular being born, growing up, growing older, dying—in a struggle for self-preservation which keeps the struggler the same only as he becomes different; which, in fact, succeeds only as it fails. Any person's history, whether he looks back upon it himself or another looks back upon it, discloses itself as a struggle to live and not die; to live on, somehow, even when dead, to *outlive* chance and sufferance, to outlive the actualities of a world not made for him and ever requiring to be made over, to be made over no less when what he is making over is already a work of his hands, called for by his heart and devised by his head.

Philosophical systems are such makings-over; world-pictures composed by means of imaginative extrapolations from the actualities of chance and sufferance and following different trajectories from the same initiations, crossing one another and tangling with one another as they shape up into their own formations. But diverse and conflicting as their histories show the systems of metaphysics, theology, paraphysics, ethics, or esthetics to be, each is offered as a demonstration or proof that the universe is such that somehow, somewhere, mankind do live in, if but vicariously, but symbolically; if but like Tantalus or Sisyphus, or like the denizens of Inferno in Dante's *Divine Comedy,* to say nothing of the denizens of Paradiso. All might be appraised as diverse and competing elaborations of the hymn,

> I'm but a stranger here,
>   Heaven is my home;
> Earth is a desert drear,
>   Heaven is my home.

It is because the philosophic world-pictures are thus diverse and competing, that the third great question gets asked perforce, How do you know? Systems of logic, theories of knowledge called epistemology are designed or developed in order to answer this question, and often the answers render knowing at once the cause and cure of being. Theories of knowledge are made to suffuse and supplant doctrines of being, each bent on vindicating the truth of this and the error of that; each reducing its competitor to a pretension to be doubted. All together keep the question, *How do you know?* urgently alive. They transvalue men's struggles for self-preservation into an ever-changing quest for certainty and for security. A major consequence of their strivings is to transfer the seat of certainty and of security from the circumambiences wherein these are sought to the heart and the head of the seeker.

The consummation is that security and certainty cease to be thought states of reliable knowledge and are held to be acts of faith. On the articles of their faiths men bet their own lives and other men's lives. They bet on them as prophecies of the future, as forecasts of the shape of things to come. Their knowings are but believings; they are present anticipations of future events.

And what else can they be if men's struggles for survival are the struggles for futurity that they are? What else can they be, if the very inwardness of their selfhood is, what as struggle it is identical with, actual insecurity, actual ambiguity and uncertainty? In these are the immediacies of our experience. These are its initiations, its *fons et origo*. It was their direct discovery that led Paul Blood to write, in his *Anaesthetic Revelation*, way back in 1874:

> Certainty is the root of despair. The inevitable stales, while doubt and hope are sisters. Not unfortunately, the universe is wild—game-flavored as a hawk's wing. Nature is miracle all. She knows no laws; the same returns not save to bring the different. The slow round of the engraver's lathe gains but the breadth of a hair, but the difference is distributed back over the whole curve, never an instant true—ever not quite.

It is of Paul Blood's *Anaesthetic Revelation* that William James wrote: "It fascinated me so weirdly that I am conscious of its having been a stepping stone in my thinking ever since." And I must confess to a like fascination, and through William James, to feeling myself a traveller on this unpaved philosophic road, whereon is abandoned the quest for that certainty and security guaranteed by a sure human destiny in a universe which is always and everywhere the same; whereon both get appraised as acts of faith, as present bets on a future which is not guaranteed in advance; whereon no bet can be a bet on a sure thing. Did not Paul of Tarsus declare long before Paul of Amsterdam, New York, that faith is the substance of things hoped for, the evidence of things not seen? And on the record, what else does anyone's security and certainty live from? What else but the commitment of the believer, not the creed or code he believes in?

Creeds and codes, philosophic or other, vary from person to person, from culture to culture, from age and place, to place and age. The faith's the thing; and as a human production, a philosopher's dialectic elaboration of the articles of it into a world-picture is but one among the endlessly varying elaborations all human beings, from the most primitive to the most sophisticated, tend to make. Wrote Chauncey Wright, together with Charles Peirce and Oliver Wendell Holmes, a friend of William James's youth: "From doing a religious duty there are no visible benefits to the agent, and from neglecting to do it, no visible evils, evident to any but himself. . . . But if immediate happiness in doing his duty, or misery in not doing it, is the ultimate sanction, then his religion is real, or a part of his character." Please note how this, even as it diverges from the conception of happiness we have from Aristotle, also confirms it.

Now, speaking in terms of my own political and social commitments, I'm disposed to discard both the liberal and the conservative classifications. The two terms have been overlaid with a mass of invidious meanings. When I am called upon to qualify my faith with labels, I'm apt to use the words *conservationist* and *libertarian*. Willy-nilly, the past can neither be preserved unaltered nor annihilated. The most and the best that can be done with it is presently so to conserve it as to enable the future which enters it, and in entering changes it, to change it toward an ever more abundant and diversifying liberty and safety for all mankind. The words *conservationist, libertarian* denote the beliefs on which I like to believe I bet my life. They signify the answers I make, in terms of my philosophic vocation, to the question: How individuals who are different from each other can best live together with each other to their joint satisfaction? I conceive that manners, morals, and politics are day-to-day tries at answering this question. And I don't need to add that the answers make an increasing and multiplying multitude never yet brought to a working consensus.

Of that multitude, the one to which I am committed might be designated, in Theodore Parker's phrase, *The American Idea*. It signifies an older and more elemental creed and code than a phrase which has become a current term in the American language—James Truslow Adams's *The American Dream*. The *Idea* is set forth in the first seven or eight propositions of the Declaration of Independence, in the Preamble to the Constitution, in the Bill of Rights, and in the succession of subsequent Amendments which confirm and protect the equal right of human beings who are different from each other and who are living together with each other, to life, liberty, and safety. The *Idea* defines government as but an instrument "to secure these rights" and subject to the improvements that will render it—wherever it is instituted—a more satisfying instrument for all concerned. The *Idea* grounds both the rights and their securing in "the laws of nature and of nature's

God." Obviously, if any specific religion need be taught in the nation's schools, the *American Idea* is specifically the national religion, which communicants of every other of the upward of two hundred and fifty cults at home in our United States are, in addition, jointly and severally committed to—that is, if they are *bona fide* Americans—as citizens.

As I read history, the philosophic faith which *The American Idea* signalizes is still as revolutionary a faith as it was when the creedally miscellaneous representatives of the thirteen colonies committed their lives, their fortunes, and their sacred honor to its support. Two maxims continue to signalize its singularity. Both are regularly repeated on coins and paper money of the land. The first is, *E Pluribus Unum*. The other is *Annuit Coeptis Novus Ordo Seclorum*, and is engraved also on the great seal of the United States. If we ever looked at our monies as often as we used them, coins and bills might remind us that America signifies a new order of the ages which takes the form of a union of the diverse; which grounds certainty and security in the struggle for survival on equal liberty and equal opportunity; which institutes democracy as an organization of liberties, "to secure these rights."

It is an ever new order because it is the negation of the old authoritarian order of power and privilege with its pharaohs, its emperors, its popes, its kings, its führers and its duces and commissars, ever reducing peoples to tools of government. It is a rejection of that old order at all times, in all places. But it is not the achievement it aspires to become. It is the faith of a commitment to an ideal, an order of open society, ever in the making, never quite made. It is a working, fighting hypothesis, the truth of which is not as self-evident as the Declaration of Independence says it is. But, on the record, it keeps verifying itself consequentially; the will and the courage of those who are committed to it embody their faith in the facts of the nation's ways; the amendments to its Constitution, the more just administration of its laws, the diversification and enrichment of its culture. If "In God we Trust" is engraved on our coins and imprinted on our greenbacks, the God must necessarily be the God of the Declaration, the God of the New Order of the Ages. This is the God of the unyielding struggle for equal liberty and equal safety for all men. As the late

Mr. Justice Jackson declared in one of his opinions: "There is no such thing as an achieved liberty; like electricity, there can be no substantial storage and it must be generated as it is enjoyed or the lights go out."

Here, in sum, is what I bet on when I confront problems of politics, manners, and morals.

2 | Education As Survival

What I am able to say here I have said before, to different companies of readers or listeners and on diverse occasions. The present one is more disturbed, more personal, and I deeply wish that I could bring an apter homage to the memory of the gracious friend and brave pioneer in the education of free men of whose labors my words are a remembrance and a celebration. Alas, that I cannot. A time comes when one's beliefs are so set that communication, however much it seems to vary, is like the replaying of an old record; and when one consoles oneself with the truism that what is reprise to one's own generation is discovery, is revelation, to the still-to-be-born ones that come after.

Thinking about William Kilpatrick as a thinker and teacher, I think all of a sudden of a question that Franklin Roosevelt put to his radio audience during one of his crucial fireside talks. It was when we were joining the long-embattled West in its resistance to

Hitler's Nazidom. For what, the President asked, is our United States going to war. Replies came in their thousands, but none told what he wanted the nation to know and to understand. He himself provided the sole suitable answer: the war we are entering on, he said, is a war for survival.

Now survival is end, warfare is means to the end. Survival is achieved as the means successfully overthrows the foe and finishes off the power wherewith he endangers survival. But the survival of *what*, of *whom*, their survival *how*, does not get said. It is taken for granted that it is the survival of ourselves as we are, wherever we are, and whenever; that this end is somehow self-evident. And it is taken for granted and self-evident regarding themselves and only themselves by all combatants everywhere. Not merely does each embattled nation assume its own survival as a goal unquestionable by God or man; all human institutions do so, however they are organized and whatever their creeds, their codes, their works and their ways. All struggle and strive to overpower and outlive rivals and competitors. None queries its own nature or identity as the power which is destined to overpower and outlive. Ever since Western man began to speculate about human nature and human destiny, and to design education so as to modify or to fulfil the one and to achieve or avert the other, this has been the philosophic first principle: It underlies Plato's *Republic* and *Laws*; it sticks out as Khrushchev's "we will bury you" in the latest Communist Book of Revelation.

Between, historians record diverse expressions—from Thomas Hobbes' "war of all against all" to Franklin Roosevelt's "war for survival." As Spinoza wrote in his *Theologico-Political Treatise* (ed. Elwes, Vol. II, Chapter XVI, p. 200):

> The power of nature is the power of God, which has a sovereign right over all things; and inasmuch as the power of nature is simply the aggregate of the powers of all her individual components, it follows that every individual has the sovereign right to do all he can; in other words the rights of the individual extend to the utmost limits of his power as it has been conditioned. Now it is the sovereign law and right of nature that each individual should endeavor to preserve itself as it is, without regard to anything but itself; therefore this sovereign law and right belongs to every in-

dividual . . . Whatsoever an individual does by the laws of its own nature it has a sovereign right to do inasmuch as it acts as it was conditioned by nature and cannot act otherwise.

Darwin's researches confirmed Spinoza's conceptions, confirmed them on a new ground. They disclosed an ongoing process of "natural selection" where all living beings alike as singulars within species, as species, and as other groupings and togethernesses, are engaged in a "struggle for survival" which the "survival of the fittest" consummates; the fittest being jointly and severally those that outlive their rivals and antagonists. Thus, to outlive is to be of the fittest.

On the whole and in the long run students of the ways of living matter, who followed Darwin, however much they may have diverged from him in this or that specification of the evolutionary process, have supported his overall conception of its dynamic. They agree that it operates in *genus humanum* as in all other animal species, and they observe that this species differs from others in that its young come to birth rather singly than in litters; that they come to birth so helpless, so utterly dependent, that without the very prolonged care by elders they would perish; that they learn from this care, and after a time without this care, from experience; and that their life-span is much longer than any other animal's. Students record still other marks distinguishing man the animal from the rest of the animal world. They note lacks—of claws and fangs; they note possessions—of hands. They appraise both lack and possession as deficiencies first of a common animality, an arrest of development, and later as sufficiencies of a common humanity. The humanization of man the animal is postulated on these deficiencies. It is achieved as the diverse and diversifying aggregations, groupings, cultures, civilizations, each a process of repetition and variation wherein, while becoming different in itself, it preserves its differential identity against others. So every individual lives on only as he changes from birth to death, yet somehow compenetrates the procession of his alterations into an ongoing identity of Selfhood.

This is why, for the descendants of Adam, survival is an ambiguous term. It can denote sheer continuing animality—the perduration of the body without regard to the body's mind, to its believings and knowings, its doings and sufferings. Such survival is known. A great many Jews perdured a thousand and one nights of Nazi concentration camps, surviving only as animal bodies, not as human persons. Yet they had not been collected, tortured, and deadened but not killed because they were animal bodies. They were collected and tortured and brought to psychical death because their identity was signified by the word Jew and its variants. Those denoted a creed and a code, a way of life and thought whence each individual called Jew was supposed to draw his cultural identity. His executioners projected this imaged identity upon his animal nature, whether or not it was realized and sustained as his personal history. It was not for this animal nature that Hitlerism designed his extinction, but for his cultural identity.

There was implied an ancient belief that man the animal and man the man are two and not one; that hence a man's animal nature can survive the extinction of his human nature, but not that his human nature can live on when his animal nature has been destroyed. The former cannot survive the latter any more than a candle's flame can continue after its candle is burned out. Human nature is an activity of animal nature as a candle's flame is the burning, indeed the burning up, of the candle. We can put out the flame without destroying the candle—so the Soviets preserve Lenin's corpse—but when the candle is all gone, the flame is gone, too. The light and warmth of our humanity come to their end in a like manner. Each human individual, we are told, consists from conception of a quantum of animal energy solidly compacted in his genes. Growing, growing up, growing older, is a sequence of patterns which the energy shapes as it spends itself and replaces what it spends (the complex of nourishment is the replacement) while at the same time its élan diminishes, its tempo slows, until at last it has used itself up and leaves the body-residue we call death. Survival as actuality is personal history, is the individual making himself; is the successive events which span the interval from conception to death, each somehow an evasion or overcoming of the mortality which besets it.

On the record, the repudiation of death as destiny, even as contingency, is intrinsic to most personal histories. The families of mankind everywhere teach their generations that only the body comes to death, that the true Self is Spirit, the ghost, the breath of life which the body's doings respire but do not constitute; that this Self survives the body and stays alive when the body has died. It is as a candle's flame would be that burns on after the candle has burned out. It is a flame that cannot burn out. Man's mortal past is his animality; his immortal past, his humanity. The families of mankind everywhere teach their generations that as human they cannot die and do not die.

This teaching is the ideal of immortality. Given diverse, often incompatible expression in every culture, it has figured as a crucial survival-value of the human struggle for survival. The endeavors to reach from the ideal to the experience which it postulates, together with what the mind actually perceives, compose a cultural heritage, a communal history of personal histories being lived out together, making their embodiments in products and establishments that survive when their makers perish. His cultural heritage man cannot account for by his animal heredity. No individual can change his own heredity: its stuff and élan is the genes whose conjunction at conception initiated his personality; and this is the case for every individual of every generation. He might affect the animal heredity of his children by choosing his mate, but only contingently, for he cannot predetermine when which sperm shall penetrate which ovum to accomplish conception. To understand a community of culture anywhere on the globe in terms of its animal heredity is not to understand it at all as humanly constituted. Its struggle for existence is a struggle for its continuance as a formation from its cultural heritage. It is the multitude of cultural formations, not the solitude of animal form which embody the significant differences among human kind.

This is why the term "race" is biologically empty and sociologically void of all meaning save as it is used to signify a configuration of the ways and works of men with one another, with the articles of faith and philosophies of culture which rationalize them. When the Nazis used the word "race" this is how they used it, elaborating a biological fiction into a cult and culture of Aryanism. The Bolsheviks used the word "class" similarly, as they diversely reworked Marx's dogma of "class-war" into the doctrines and disciplines of Sino-Russian's Communism. Re-formations of this kind start in an act of faith. Whatever else the formulae define, they do not define *Homo sapiens* the biological fact. As such a fact, male and female from any "race" or any "class" can and do mate and reproduce their kind. All are alike individuals of the human "race," alike branches of a common heredity expressing itself in all the world's categories of *homo sap*. As humans, their survival is cultural, not biological.

It is a truism that there are modes of cultural survival. One mode is perduration without growth. It is not the same as physical survival, since the latter comprises a certain sequence of bodily changes which growing-up consists of. Survival without growth is cultural survival. It is the upkeep of a way of life by a society of human beings whose generations only repeat the past, living out their lives as their parents have lived out theirs, professing the same creeds, following or evading the same codes in the same ways, eating the same foods, drinking the same drinks, loving and hating, working and playing, fighting and praying as their ancestors used to, with the same words, the same tools, the same weapons, the same rites and the same rotes.

Primitives, whom anthropologists study—say aborigines in Australia or Africa or the Americas—do so live in a very great degree. Primitives whom writers like Faulkner take for figures in their narratives, such as the Hillbillies of the piedmont of Virginia, the Carolinas, or Kentucky, or the Klans and White Citizens' Councils of Mississippi, do so live in a very great degree, repeating the ancestral folkways and mores, "the Southern way of life." For them, survival is this repetition. It is the kind of survival the mythopoeic Arnold Toynbee attributed to the Jews. He called the Jewish culture a fossil culture, the Judaist religion a fossil religion. "Fossil" didn't designate a dead skeleton. I gather that Toynbee intended it to mean a formation passively alive, lacking both the capacity and the will to the active living which is growth—a culture and religion repeating generation after generation the works and faith of the forefathers.

Anthropologists do report on cultures that might be qualified as "fossil." They occur in various formations relating to the difference between the circumstances affecting their survival.

Some circumstances may work as isolators. By chance or choice, people may get shut away from all contact, all communication with other people of a different culture. The isolated culture would thereupon become repetitive, turn in on itself, lose its vital impulsion, harden, and become what the word "fossil" may have implied to Toynbee. Isolation is sometimes imposed, as Christian power endeavored to impose it on the Jews, as the South Africans and Mississippians endeavor to impose it on their Negroes. This mode of isolation is rarely complete, hardly ever successful. As everybody knows, both Jews and Negroes not only maintained contact with their environments of culture, they extended by absorbing from them ideas and ideals, attitudes and thoughts and methods that modified, even displaced, the cultural heritage they had received from their fathers. So nourished, the latter grew and diversified; it did not fossilize.

Sometimes isolation is imposed by States as well as churches. Sometimes the isolator is a combination of church and state, such as still sustains the Indian caste-system with its order of "untouchables" shut out and cut off from all communication that might alter the way of life whereby the generations of "untouchables" are identified. Their culture is fossilized and their survival is a fossil survival because they are excommunicated from what is culturally different.

By means of a coerced or self-imposed excommunication families of mankind can maintain a religion or a culture unaltered from without and, by inference, from within. Cultures so surviving would lack any real history, since history is real only as it exhibits differences within the past, differentiation of the present from the past, and the future as an alteration of both. Real history consists in the present transformation of the past: its present is ever the remaking of the past by the future. This remaking, personal or interpersonal, is the substance of living as human, the stuff of history, the ongoing *Now* of man's survival as man.

The more common word for this ongoing *Now* is growth. Neither as flesh nor as spirit can we truly survive without growing. All flesh grows in patterned sequences. Animals are born, they mature, they age, they die. So does the human animal, but he takes, let me repeat, very much longer stretches of time. His physical infancy is longer, so are the periods of maturation into sexual potency, of ripening into bodily adulthood, of slow slackening into the deficiencies and ineptnesses of old age, until the fires of life have burned down into the ashes of death. Everybody's body lives this succession of changes, even the idiot's. But the idiot lives them with no succession of mental changes, with no growth of the mind to speak of. People can impose idiocy on other people; on a religious or a scientific communion, on a province, on a nation, by allowing for a multiplication of numbers but preventing any diversification of the articles of faith, the vision and the works which together shape up into the spirit or culture of the group or society in question.

Now the matrix of the divergence of human from animal survival is the human animal's capacity for learning. Non-human animals also have this capacity but in so limited a range that the quantitative amounts to a qualitative difference. Most species have very little; their struggle for survival is prevailingly instinctual. Some can acquire a few tricks, like a horse, a dog, a monkey and a variety of circus animal but they cannot devise ways to overcome crises, nor are they capable of producing the enormous changes of themselves and of the world around them which signalize the human struggle for survival. The humanity of the human animal may be said to manifest itself as these changes and, in view of them, as its unbounded capacity to learn. Except for this capacity, men are not born human. At birth men are animals. They achieve humanity by learning—first in the family scene, then in the school, then in the near and then the farther circumambience. They learn ways of feeling, talking and acting, creeds and codes as professions, in articulated behaviors as practices. They learn from an indefinite variety of persons by personal contact; from images of persons and portrayals of events by imaginative perception. What they learn combines with them to form cultural types. To grow up and grow old as a human being is to enter into the formation of a cultural type. It is to shape oneself, say, into a farmer, an industrial worker, a doctor, a lawyer, a priest, an engineer, a politician, a saint, a confidence man, and so on. Whatever occupation parents may have, their children are not born endowed with them. To grow up into them, they must learn them.

Occupations and interests are acquired characteristics; that which constitutes them, that which learning achieves, is an insight into a selected and particular part of the circumambient world. If, for example, a boy is to become a doctor, he becomes one by first of all frequenting places that doctors frequent—places such as medical schools and libraries and hospitals and doctors' offices. He reads medical books, he learns medical lingo, he handles medicine's materials and tools. He repeats medical beliefs and behaviors, until the whole aggregate has become a formation which it is his life to master, to act in freely, easily, with assurance. Then he is a good doctor, he has made himself a skillful and imaginative user of the places, the tools and the materials wherewith doctoring is constituted. The luxury of his offices and the numbers of his staff are irrelevant. Only his knowledge and skill in the uses of these things and places to heal the sick, and to keep the healthy in health are relevant. The "better" the doctor the freer and more at home he is in the region of his circumambience called the science and art of medicine. Its configurations *are* his medical mind.

Similarly a lawyer, a musician or teacher. A lawyer *is* a lawyer in so far as he freely and masterfully finds his way in the region of his surroundings which the "law" signifies—the law schools, the law courts, the law offices, their literature, all the doings they call for and impattern. They constitute his legal mind.

A person is said to have a musical mind when he is at home and free in that region of his circumambience which "music" signifies—the region of scores of all kinds, of musical instruments in and out of use, of human voices, of orchestras, of virtuosos, of "live" and recorded performances, of compositions, of musicians' unions and other associations defining themselves by musical interests, all of them together shaping up into the region of a culture which "music" spans.

So the mind of a teacher is denoted by the range and depth of his area of knowledge, the freedom, ease and sureness with which he moves about in it, his insight into the actualities of how pupils may best learn what he has to teach them, his sense of his role in the total economy of schooling. A good teacher is one from whom those that he teaches so learn that they come to quest for themselves a freedom and ease like his own of the field of knowledge he leads them into. He becomes the Jones they aspire to keep up with.

With ever-arising variations, a similar dynamic sustains the formation of every sort and condition of mind in the cultures of mankind. A person's mind is constituted by *what* he minds, and with what satisfaction and consequence he minds it. His survival as this person and not that is an ongoing process of selective minding. In so far as success may be ascribed to it, it initiates, it nourishes and it sustains an ordered yet changeful configuration of ideals and events, values and existences. The ideals or values design a working, fighting faith which impatterns events, existences, persons and places in an order of importance, a structure of priorities for survival. Call the impatterning act of faith a person's perduring *I* or *Self*, then the thoughts, things and happenings which it impatterns become his *Me*. *I* and *Me* relate to one another as focus and fringe, point-of-view and horizon. Not infrequently the components of *Me*, and occasionally of *I*, change status and function. A person lives on as their orchestration. In his characterization by himself or by others, now this component is taken for dominant, now that; which follows from the problematical situation that calls forth the resolving characterizations. Such words as *democrat, totalitarian, libertarian, authoritarian, American, Russian, Briton, Chinese,* and each and every other term that people employ to qualify and define one another, signifies a selection from the unbounded multitude compounding into the singulars which struggle for self-preservation.

The humanity of mankind, then, is jointly and severally not one but many. Its civilization is a plurality of singular cultures each different from the others and struggling for its own survival among the others. Each willy-nilly works and fights to maintain its own identity, to win support for it from the others, or to defend it from their rivalry and aggression, so that it may live on among them and outlive them if it can. The innermost citadel of its struggle is the formation of its young in the image of their elders; in securing such a commitment to the identity—the *I-Me*—which the image portrays that each generation will continue it as the Self unalienable to all the generations, ever to be worked and striven for so that it shall outlive all the others that it struggles among for survival. In one word, the innermost citadel of its struggle is education.

As the diversity, range and scope of our American educational establishment manifest, and as the dimensions of its economy testify, the American people have been more aware than other peoples of this fact of life as human. They have relied less than others upon the unconscious and undesigned learnings whereby the ages to come repeat the ages that have gone before. They have examined and reshaped these into the conscious and purposeful endeavors of which their school systems are the vehicles, and other societies, servile even more than free, have taken them for their Joneses of education, aspiring not only to keep up with them, but to outdistance them. It may still be said, as H. G. Wells said long ago that American education is the grand design of Americanization.

Suffusing all the formations of the mind enabled by the specific sciences of nature and man invidiously called "humanities" and by the specific arts and vocations, there is the American Idea, with its derivative, the American Dream. Idea and Dream signify a doctrine or creed which the Declaration of Independence utters, a discipline or code which the Constitution of the United States designs. In all schools, elementary, high, cultural, vocational, in all colleges and universities, all institutions of adult study, the doctrine gets somehow reaffirmed, the discipline somehow redefined by their compenetration with the singular thinkings and doings and things and events which, as they are learned, becomes the learner's mind. The design is that it may become a mind, which singly or in company with others, will fit a free society of free men such as the American Idea envisions and American aspiration keeps struggling to embody, to diversify and to perfect.

That this struggle is arduous, bitter, tearful, often bloody and exhausting, no historian disputes. That it is progressively successful, authorities of the social sciences join historians in disputing. And in recent years the knowing as well as the naive, the judicious as well as the prejudiced among the nation's pundits of opinion have charged the nation's schools with uses of freedom that defeat instead of advancing freedom's survival. As scapegoats for this guilty use of freedom, they have selected the most representative translators of the American Idea into a theory and practice of education for Americans, if not for mankind everywhere. They charge to John Dewey and William Kilpatrick all the errors, actual and fancied, that they can enumerate—of course, with no regard to the plight of the schools nor to the circumambient influences amid which what they appraise as bad arises. This is like charging traffic accidents to the rules of the road instead of violation of the rules.

For the import of the rules is that the littlest and flimsiest vehicle equally with the most gargantuan in size and horsepower shall reach its own stopping place on its own power in the quickest, freest, safest way. The rules of the road are rules of survival for different travellers as different. And what Dewey initiated and Kilpatrick diversified, and both have striven for, is such a reconstruction of the rules of the road called learning, as the state of the sciences of man and nature, and of their use by the industrial and fine arts, could at the time, enable. Neither philosopher of education assumed that this state was always and everywhere the same and would not change. Far from it. Their reconstructions stemmed from their recognizing as their opponents did not, that in the course of events some truths would be reappraised as errors, some tools and skills would be displaced by others better suited to the perennial tasks of a people struggling to survive as a free society of free men. They recognized, as their opponents did not, that surviving thus is accomplished in a formation of changing configurations of faith, wisdom and works diversifying, and compounding as they diversify. They recognized, as their opponents did not, that the American Idea is at once the design, the matrix and the symbol of this surviving.

Perhaps they also recognized—here I may be attributing to them my own perceptions and beliefs (to me truisms difficult indeed to persuade others of)—that this struggle to go on struggling is an alteration of both the personal and the interpersonal past. Consider the selves we feel we are, believe we are, or know we are as we know perceptually and analytically that which other things are. How do we experience our individual identity, know it, understand it? Certainly we each of us sense it as *passage*, as feelings, perceptions, ideas, images, mingled and streaming on *now*, signalized by a perduring name, with a warm intimacy of meaning beyond any other name purely because it is one's own name. But should we strive to span with this *now* whatever we were and felt and did ten years ago, twenty years ago, back to our infancy, as psychoanalysis strives, we should not prehend any ongoing same, any constant identity recurring, recollection for recollection. If we possessed photographs of ourselves taken on successive days through the years of our lives and could lay them out in their calendar order we would perceive them not as successive pictures of the selfsame person but as ongoing differentiations from a same. If we nevertheless realized an identity, it would not be the same repeating itself, but the succession of differents compenetrating, suffusing each the others, identifying themselves with one another. One's self, then, is not an unchanging identity but an activity of differents in such reciprocal identification that each successive variation suffuses and modifies those which came before, and alters and increases the past they have become: all the *thens* of our existence *now* are thus somehow present in this latest *now*. They are our living past, and so the stuff of our present Selves. As living, Self is the past changing and growing; that is, presently altered by the deliberate or instant acts of choice or decision whereby the future, *now* passing into the past, diversifies it. To live, to grow up, to grow older in culture and the spirit is thus ongoingly to change one's past. The aptest word for this activity is learning: it signifies humanity ever remaking itself. It signifies man's struggle to preserve himself which he wins only as he alters himself. To stay as is, not to alter, is to fossilize.

Now the learning, self-altering, Self is related to *what* it learns in two obvious ways. One is the way of competition, rivalry and strife. Whether spontaneously or by intention, it joins this or that circumambience to the Self as enemy, human or non-human. Survival requires learning the foe's nature, vital needs, ways of satisfying them, and whatever else he attributes survival-values to; it requires a use of what has been learned to devise strategies and skills of defense and of attack. This is the understanding that Plato had in mind when he defined courage as wisdom concerning dangers. The requirements for survival amid the traffic of a modern city might be called such a wisdom. For to make one's way safely and surely among the vehicles on, say, New York's streets, one must needs compound into a habit: watching and readiness, knowing the rules of the road, the meanings of traffic signals, the powers and pleasures of traffic cops, the variations of going and stopping among different vehicles. The compenetration of all this into a personal disposition is a wisdom concerning a certain variety of danger, such as Safety Councils would like school children to learn. But because survival is a struggle going on, because its significance is ever consequential, ever future, because on occasion we must needs keep moving, whatever the rules and the lights, whoever the traffic cop, this wisdom is not enough. Survival may call for risking extinction, for betting our lives on an instant perception of thoroughfare with no hedging and no likely prospect of winning. Or survival may permit calculated risks: courage might then be defined as the wisdom of calculated risks.

If these varieties of courage are crucial for individuals making private choices, they are momentous for individuals making public ones, individuals choosing for groups—for institutions, peoples, states or cultures. Decisions on rites and rotes, on issues of state at home or abroad are regularly takings of calculated risks, the calculations being based on informations called "intelligence," and the decisions assuming that the intelligence is reliable and being used rightly at the right time. Their matter and manner are learnings; they are processes and products of survival. We measure their survival-value by the issue we bet on. Against some opponents the stake is existence itself: they fight not simply to outlive us, but to do so by destroying us. Others strive not to destroy us but to outdo us, to do the same thing we are doing more simply, more excellently, at less cost, with less effort, and by so outdoing, to outlive us. On the record such strivers would seem to be necessary to each others' learning and growth. A different species of opponent strives both to outdo his antagonist and to finish him off by outdoing him. Wisdom concerning dangers recognizes these differences and with what skill and knowledge each might be overcome.

In modern parlance, wisdom so understood is survival, it is "the courage to be" recognized as the unceasing diversification and reciprocal suffusion of the sciences and the arts. Our survival is their growing, their growing as learning. In brief, survival is education, education is survival.

Certain truisms follow. Experience educates us independently of any art or science; *ad hoc* establishments educate us on purpose—with an art, a science and rationalizing philosophy of education as the means thereto—deciding the *what* and the *how* of our learning. Learning should transform our past beliefs and behaviors into faiths and works whose consequences are more satisfying, more successful survival. Teaching should facilitate this perduring alteration of the past, invest it with direction, goals and methods. It should but it rarely does. For the most part, a teacher's assigned task is symbolically to repeat in the young the past of their elders, intact, and in such wise that they will seek to have the same things repeated in *their* young. By and large, among all the peoples on the globe the teaching art has been an art of fossilization. John Dewey and William Kilpatrick have been, each in his way, pioneers of the endeavor to transform and transvalue this part of the educational enterprise. They were at once rebels and discoverers and innovators who strove to displace fossilization by liberation and growth, and they so figure in the history of education, however the historians appraise their educational faith and works.

Because of Kilpatrick, because of Dewey, their partisans and foes alike recognize that education is a process first of the formation or *re*formation of beliefs, and then of the fixation of beliefs. When beliefs have become so fixed that the believer cannot help affirming and acting on them, his character has set, his life has been committed in such wise that he is apt to appraise persons who differ from him as deficient in culture, in virtue, in wisdom. He is apt to consign them to an Outgroup of the lesser human, to treat them as somehow "untouchable," and to require their assent to his appraisal of them.[1] There are other words for education which such fixing of belief consummates. They are *instruction*,

---

[1] So Soviet educators have described Dewey and Kilpatrick as chauvinists and servants of American capitalist imperialism, formers of a generation of servants of this imperialism, conscienceless foes of true intelligence and morality—of course as modes of only Communist survival.

inculcation, indoctrination, discipline. Americans commonly use
the last two in qualifying military education; but they figure also
as traditional to "classical" or "liberal" education. They have been
especially expressive of the teaching in religious establishments.
As employed to form and fix the future by transforming or suppressing the past, they have currently gained a synonym: "brainwashing." And indeed it would be in no way incorrect to say that
to indoctrinate and discipline a person is ultimately to "brain-
wash" him, to disable him from examining and choosing alternatives of faith or works. Such disablement is implicit in *instruction*
and *inculcation* as well. All four methods of teaching are methods
which so change a learner as to put an end to change. They render all schools, be they seminaries for sub-debs or institutes of the
higher technologies, literally finishing schools where drill and
other such devices are employed to fix beliefs beyond any unfix-
ing. When successful, they *are* brainwashing. They render alternatives intolerable, considering them fraught with pain and evil.
If attention to them can't be avoided, it is suffused with annoy-
ance, weakened by impatience, displaced by anger, even by rage;
and ultimately by violence against whoever effected the confrontation. This frame of mind has been perennial in religious societies.
Whether supernaturalist or naturalist, sacerdotal or secular, they
manifested it in their censorships, their heresy-trials, their inquisi-
tions and *autos-da-fé*. It is a differentia of fossilized cultures.

Kilpatrick, following Dewey, was an American, the foremost
of our times in the United States not only, but wherever the education of free men became a vital concern, in working out an
alternative method of forming and fixing belief. Like Dewey, he
postulated equal liberty and equal opportunity to learn for all the
generations of youth; like Dewey, he postulated the perceptions
and findings of the new psychologies of man derived from Darwin's conclusions regarding the origin of species and the descent
of man. He was not unaware that both would be undergoing alterations in this aspect or that, as the frontiers of the sciences of
nature and man were pushed back; that some of the beliefs with
which he worked would be displaced by others which could do
the same job more successfully. But he firmly believed also that
the new insights regarding the act of learning that supervened on

those of Woodward and Thorndike—say the insights of the Gestaltist and the psychoanalysts and their epigones would still confirm the initiating postulates, however much the confirmations might diverge from each other. With Dewey, Kilpatrick recognized that the humanity of the human animal consists in its being a learner, hence an animal instinct with curiosity, looking, listening, peeking, prying, breaking up, putting together, fancying, consuming, producing, and—remembering, as its hungers and thirsts and lusts prompt and their facilitations and frustrations stir its curiosity and shape and signalize its satisfactions. Because this is what distinguishes the man-animal from other animal species, man becomes a discoverer of what already exists and a creator of what does not yet exist; he discards earlier discoveries and creations for later ones which for the nonce serve better his self-altering struggle to go on struggling that is his existence. His discoveries and creations may or may not satisfy him: he keeps tasting and testing them all for satisfactoriness. If they meet his tests, he commits himself to their survival; he ordains them as values of his. Commitment is a closure of any process of inquiry or creation, of any innovation or development. Commitment is a fixation of belief.

After commitment, creation is succeeded by reproduction, innovation by repetition, curiosity turns in a new direction, toward a newly imagined goal. For the sciences, however, commitment, satisfying as may be the reproductions that ensue upon it, is experimental and temporary; fixed beliefs obtain only as working hypotheses, ever open to revision or displacement.

But when, in or out of the sciences, a belief is fixed beyond revision or displacement, be the results of experience, experiment and verification what they may, commitment ceases to be scientific or reasonable and becomes religious and creedal. That is, the believer sticks to his belief regardless of consequences; he takes its content for a matter of "ultimate concern," he bets his life on it, as Job was believed to bet his life (according to the classical perversion of the fifteenth verse of the thirteenth chapter: "Though he slay me, will I trust in him."). So the believer dies trusting. So martyrs die, choosing to give up their lives rather than give up their beliefs. So mankind commits itself to any object of belief, as Tertullian did to the crucial doctrine of the Christian gospel of salvation—the death and resurrection of Christ—writing, *Credo quia absurdum est, certum est quia impossible est.*

Tertullian was taking this doctrine for a matter of "ultimate concern" and making an absolute commitment. Although our own age has witnessed the insurgence of such commitments in Nazism, in the Fascisms, and in varieties of Communism, and although they repeat in certain secular and sacerdotal supernaturalisms, the absolutism is self-limiting. The modern part of the contemporary world regards it as suicidal, not survivalist; its mind is spoken in Mark Twain's theorem: "Faith is believing what you know ain't so," and in Josh Billings' scholium: "It is better to know nothing than to know what ain't so."

Here the alternatives present an issue which can be said to have been the matrix of Dewey's inquiries into matters of "ultimate concern" and of Kilpatrick's differentiations between science and philosophy and his genial application of those working hypotheses to the educator's art. Although one can note reservations, both teachers of teachers had become poignantly aware that the human career had turned largely on believing what it later found "ain't so;" that if the formation of mankind's humanity is at all a struggle for survival, it can't be better to know nothing than to know what ain't so. For the history of civilization is a history of sciences and arts and crafts all compact of truths which, because of later discoveries, creations and inventions, have been demoted from truths to errors, from skills to ineptitudes. For civilization is a sequence of displacements of earlier beliefs by later ones that do better for the struggle to go on struggling which diversifies into the cultures of mankind. But when peoples cling and insist on clinging to the ancestral beliefs and on indoctrinating their descendants with them, regardless of the superior survival-value of the later ones actually experienced, then they make of education the limitation, not the enlargement of survival.

Kilpatrick, following Dewey, saw that the issue—limitation or enlargement—centered rather on the *how* than the *what* of the educative process. It centers on method. And it centers on method because the *what* consists of whatever faiths and works the powers of the place and time direct the teacher to teach. If the method is such as to render openness of mind habitual, so that the

learner believes and understands that what he now knows and relies on might later be transformed or displaced by more reliable
learnings, then education enlarges survival, survival is enlarging
education. But if teaching fixes in the learner's belief that *what* he
has learned is inalterable and eternal, if teaching thus stops growth
and arrests change, education is limitation of survival. Let, therefore, the *what* be what content of the past it may, the *how* of
education must be a cultivation of curiosity, a formation of interests, an exploration of the *what* that takes it apart and puts it together again symbolically and materially. A learner so taught will
be in his studies a discoverer, an innovator, an experimenter
whose trials and errors test what he discovers or invents, and
whose research and examination of alternatives, whose communication with rivals and competitors, check the findings of his tests.
He will not be merely repeating the past he studies, he will be
altering it with new values and new meanings vital to himself.
Kilpatrick's "project method" seems to me designed to satisfy
these requirements for the *how* of the education of free men for
survival. Critics have appraised it exclusively in terms of recorded
incompetent and unsuccessful employments of it. Nevertheless, if
any method more apt to the end-in-view has been proposed, I am
not aware of it.

In relation to the past of Western mankind, the West of this
twentieth century might well be qualified as not a development
but a mutation. Henry Adams, reporting upon his personal history as his education, remarked emphatically that there is a
greater difference of spirit and culture between a man born in
1900 C.E. and one born in 1800 C.E., than between a man born in
1800 C.E. and one born in 800 B.C.E. He attributed the difference to
the new *how* and the new *what* which give its specific identity to
the mind of today's West. These are the *how* and *what* of the
democratic image of man and the democratic ideal of human relations, and of the principles and practices of pure and applied science.

The first postulates that people are singulars different by nature and hence by right; that the different are equal in rights and
hence that to suffer penalties or assume privileges for difference

has no ground in nature and should have no warrant in law; that all societies, however large or small, whatever their other purposes, are unions of differents formed in order to assure to one another equal liberty, safety and opportunity.

The second postulates all that the phrase "modern science" intends and connotes, together with all that in the economy of labor and leisure is signified by the expressions "first industrial revolution," "second industrial revolution," "automation," "urbanization," "mass culture" and the like.

The two together compose an unprecedently innovative intellectual, political and cultural economy wherein the temporal and spatial distances between peoples and persons are so contracted that the very continents have been called neighborhoods and their human inhabitants neighbors, able to visit with one another and to learn from one another in ever greater numbers. Sequent on this mounting change is an image which joins all the peoples of the world into one free society of free men, a cooperative, self-orchestrating union of mankind. The articles of faith defining this image are written into the Universal Declaration of Human Rights. The program of works that should establish the faith as fact are the Charter of the United Nations Organization, and of the United Nations Scientific Educational and Cultural Organization, each with its diverse organs and agencies. Together, they look for an education wherewith all would assure to each his survival in equal liberty and equal security.

But, as against the faith and the program of works, we must set the record of the war of all against all within the circumambience of the new global economy; we must hold in mind that the new nearnesses have largely facilitated old rivalries and engendered new ones, from competitions for excellence to wars of annihilation with weapons of annihilation; we must be alert to the condition that communications by means of the new media are directed far more largely against the orchestral union of the different than on its behalf. Dewey and Kilpatrick's teachings about education as ideal and as program are being disputed and discarded on behalf of the ancestral authoritarian indoctrination and disciplining which, they had given proof, can contribute little to the survival of a free society of free men. Patriots with a care for education, professional and non-professional both, look with dread and alarm upon the achievements of scientists under authoritarian communism and bid Americans reform the nation's educational establishments in emulation of the Russians whom they have taken for their Jones to keep up with in education. The issue they raise returns education to alternatives of choice more tragic even than those of a hundred years ago, during dark, dark days of our Civil War, when Abraham Lincoln told the nation: "The dogmas of the quiet past are inadequate to the stormy present. The occasion is piled high with difficulty, and we must rise to the occasion. As our case is new, so we must think anew. We must disenthrall ourselves, and then we shall save our country."

I have lost count of the number of times I have called attention to these words of Lincoln's. I do so again, in this remembrance of William Kilpatrick, because I deeply believe that, concerning the education of free men he, with Dewey, was a pioneer of disenthrallment. It is right, it is fitting, that all of us who have a care for the survival of free society through the education of free men should recall in reverence the daring spirits who led the pioneering.

3 "Color-Blind"

Perhaps the anecdote is a parable. Perhaps it is a true story. Perhaps it is both. It was told, "with pride," by a Southern Senator, just back in Washington from a visit home, to a Senator from the Far West. Its hero is a little boy whom the story-teller met coming from his now "integrated"—that is, all-American—school, in the company of a Negro classmate. The statesman had stopped to ask the boy how he was enjoying school, and the boy had answered: "Just fine. This is my friend, Willie, and he doesn't seem to mind that I am white."[1]

[1] Bel Kaufman, listing high school student comments on "Integration" (p. 216 of *Up the Down Staircase*) records a match for this: "I have this colored friend, Betty, well I never thought about it one way or the other, until one day I went over to her house for the first time and her father opened the door and I was surprised to see he was colored. Because, to me, I was so used to her, she always looked normal." A more reflective expression of the sentiment is the comment of a white lawyer of a public agency on the stress laid by a New York Negro newspaper on his color. He said that "white" was being used as prejudiciously as "black."

41

The story assumes, of course, that neither did the white boy mind that Willie was black. They were friends, and friends can be friends only as equals: there may be love and good will between unequals, as between parents and children, humans and animals, employers and employees, masters and slaves, but there cannot be friendship. Not-minding can be interpreted in more than one way, and in most, friendship is not the bond.

Such not-minding, as it is the bond of, is the earliest and most natural. It is the way of children before they have been "socialized" by acquiring the impassioned prejudices which animate their elders and learning the doctrines and disciplines which are used to rationalize them. It is this process of "socialization" that led Voltaire long ago to observe: *"Credidi propter quod locutus sum*—I believe it because I have said it—is the motto of mankind; they repeat an absurdity, and by dint of repeating it become persuaded of it."* But the wont and use of young children is for each to take all others as they come, skin-color and all, to play and study with, eat and drink and rest with, to be friends and rivals with, on equal terms. Trained observers tell how small children regularly take all their companions on their own level, accepting their diversities, as equal partners in their doings: this is to say that for children, difference is, in the language of the political philosophers, a natural right, the same for all the differents—for white differing from white and black differing from black, as well as for white differing from black and black differing from white. And natural rights are, like breathing, vital functions without which life cannot long go on; they may be contained or expanded, reduced or enhanced, but they can be eliminated only by eliminating the individual or the group whose functions they are. This is why natural rights are recognized as "unalienable" and as the roots and sanctions of all other rights. Growing up, growing older, entangles them in struggles of self-defense against efforts at alienation—alienation by force, alienation by fraud. An individual's biography, a people's history—whatever the colors they are labeled by, and whether conventionally one or actually many— tells the story of such struggles. The vital spring of events in both personal and interpersonal history is struggle against attempts to alienate the unalienable.

The struggle takes on many shapes, of which one is a way of not-minding, a way that becomes visible wherever sundry traits of any sort or condition of our strivings to keep existing get treated as signalizing a personal or group identity and their possessors get penalized for possessing them. In the conscience of the latter the traits are thereby devalued into weaknesses or defects which hamper, even cripple, their endeavors to go on striving toward a free, safer, more abundant future: endeavors of which each person's struggle for survival is the union. Individuals and groups strain every which way to change this identification, to rid themselves of the identifying traits, at least in appearance. If they cannot improve or overcome, they suppress; they ignore; they deny; or they transvalue; they purport to cherish overt weakness as covert virtue, bespoken defect as secret excellence, manifest anxiety as hidden valor. They deeply desire not to see that which is as it is, and though aware of its existence and force, they purpose to blind themselves to the real presence. They pretend that refusing to acknowledge it empties it of its power in the shaping of their lives.

Cases of such not-minding are to be found in every walk of life. They are more readily visible, although less intense, in open, pluralistic societies with cultural freedom—the United States make up such a society—than in monolithic closed societies with authoritarian cultures, such as nazi, fascist, and communist rulers undertake to impose on their countrymen by secret and public policing.[2] It is a truism that the very openness and diversifications of free societies permit the safe organization of groups whose principles and practices would abolish the liberties they insist on for themselves so that they might eventually forbid them to others. Divergent instances of such formations in our United States are the American Nazi Party, the American Communist

---

[2] Free societies are still news; closed societies are old hat. Remember Aristotle: "The tyrant in order to hold his power suppresses every superiority, does away with good men, forbids education and light, controls every movement of the citizens and keeps them under perpetual control, wants them to grow accustomed to baseness and cowardice, has spies everywhere to listen to what is said in meetings and spreads dissention and calumny among the citizens and impoverishes them, is obliged to make war in order to keep his subjects occupied and impose on them the permanent need of a chief."

Party, the John Birch Society, the National States Rights Party, the White Citizens' Councils, the Ku Klux Klan, the Daughters of the American Revolution. But most of this kind join together and fall apart with their particular occasions. As history tells it, they are short-lived: their aggressive lusts swell up and subside without shaping a tradition. At most they adopt and degrade, by the meanings they give them, ancient symbols like the Christian cross or the pagan swastika. Be what may the opposition to the free society which permits and protects it, the creed and code of freedom, openness, diversity and diversification keep gaining in scope and application not only at home. As Thomas Jefferson told the young nation in his first inaugural address:

> During these contests of opinion through which we have passed, the animation of discussions and of exertions has sometimes worn an aspect which might impose on strangers unused to think freely and to speak and write what they think; but this being now decided by the voice of the nation, announced according to the rules of the Constitution, all will, of course, arrange themselves under the will of the law, and unite in common effort for the common good. All too, will bear in mind that though the will of the majority in all cases is to prevail, that will to be rightful must be reasonable; that the minority possess their equal rights which equal law must protect, and to violate would be oppression . . . And let us reflect that, having banished from our land that religious intolerance under which mankind so long bled and suffered, we have yet gained little if we countenance a political intolerance as despotic, as wicked, and capable of as bitter and bloody persecutions. . . . We are all Republicans, we are all Federalists. If there be any among us who would wish to dissolve this Union or to change its republican form, let them stand undisturbed as monuments to the safety with which error of opinion may be tolerated where reason is left free to combat it.

Neither Jefferson nor any later American champion of this principle held that it was also applicable to the use of force. Where it is confronted by "a clear and present danger" of violence—the launching of the Civil War is an outstanding instance —the true believers in equal liberty cannot in conscience fail to defend it. The totalitarian argument—first advanced to justify claims of a church to exercise power over the conscience of men —which tells lovers of liberty that logical consistency requires them to guarantee the enemies of liberty safety in destroying liberty, is a sophistical fraud. It is tantamount to arguing that commitment to liberty is commitment to its extinction, commitment to self-slaughter by the free. When violence threatens, the fruit of non-resistance is subjection which, when that which is threatened is liberty, is the same as extinction.[3] But short of any "clear and present danger," free societies do not fight out the conflicts of interest which arise at home and abroad; they talk them out, reason them out; they aim at what is being currently called "consensus," what I have long preferred to call the orchestration of the different, their teamplay based on their participation in the play as equals in liberty and rights. Law, in democratic societies, works as a series of covenants of the different, by the different, for the different; it signalizes an organization of liberty.

The diversities which unite in such an organization are of all kinds, shapes and sizes, with the elemental unit of each the individual in his singularity. Those whose identifying differential is antagonism to equal liberty are few among a multitude identified by cults and cultures, languages, ethnic derivations, sports, occupations, professions, race, color. In America all, in one specification or another, got figured as undesirable, and have been variously penalized. By and large the desirable was imaged as "white, Protestant, Anglo-Saxon," although in fact a composite of selected descendants of not always savory English, Welsh, Scotch, Scotch-Irish who together made up the peoples of the United Kingdom, and whose rival ways, creeds and cults distilled into the criteria of who belongs and who doesn't belong. When the flow of immigrants from all Europe and much of Asia—Africans were not immigrants; they were brought as unwilling captives to be sold for chattel slaves—grew large enough to render the diversities visible alternatives to the ways and works and rites and rotes of the descendants of the earlier settlers, the latters' image came to

[3] Jefferson, writing to Madison in 1787 from France: "What country can preserve its liberties if its rulers are not warned from time to time that this people preserve the spirit of resistance? Let them take arms. The remedy is to set them right as to the facts, pardon and pacify them. What signify a few lives lost in a country or two? The tree of liberty must be refreshed from time to time with the blood of patriots and tyrants. It is the natural manure."

be used as the authentic portrait of the authentic American. Those who did not fit the image were different, and therefore unequal. They must either conform to it or cheerfully accept the penalties which difference straightway incurs by submitting to their betters and doing the nation's work as they were required or permitted. So, they would become "Americanized."

Only, becoming "Americanized" also had, and continues to have, quite other meanings. One is an intent of the word "naturalization." It includes a strong urge to become a citizen of the Republic and a formal application to be admitted to citizenship. It includes—as unhappily it does not for the-native-born who, unless they are Negroes or Indians, are privileged, simply because they happen to have been born in the land, to enter into citizenship without the formal preparation required by law of the foreignborn—five years of life and labor in the land, of which study and reflection on the propositions of the Declaration of Independence and the articles and amendments of the Constitution which state the nation's creed and the nation's code are essentials. "Naturalization" is presumably consummated in a solemn public eremony: the postulant takes the oath of allegiance and, without violence to his integrity and worth as *this* person and no other, duly and in good order becomes an American citizen, equal under the law to all other citizens in his rights and liberties—be the latters' ancestry, religion, knowledge, skills and associations what they may.

In the eyes of the nation's fundamental law, then, human persons become authentic Americans either by birth or by faith. The newborn, it is presumed, grow into this faith as they grow up, without need to study or reflect; the new citizen, *per contra*, must needs do both and avow the faith, together with his readiness to bet his life on it, publicly, in the rite of naturalization. As a matter of fact, both the native and the naturalized Americans are different persons who hold the same faith. The faith it is that identifies them as Americans: other traits are either contingent or derivative and secondary, and as recent events have made sufficiently clear, may be antagonistic. Both the committed and the opposed have been described as agonists of the American Dream, but the commitment of the committed is not to any shared Dream, but to what is more correctly signalized as the American Idea.

Now the identification of the American by his readiness to bet his life on the American Idea makes quite obviously a very different identity from that which is composed of ancestry, religion, and other items drawn from the culture or value-system he grew up in. The relation between the two modes of identification is external and contingent, not organic and internal. The second is exclusive and monopolistic; it shuts out and cuts off the different; it denies that they can be equal as different; it insists that difference can only separate, not bring together; that if equality is sought, the seeking is permissible only in separation, and that the equality can be only a sameness of conditions, not of persons in their unalienable diversities. Protagonists of the second, although professing faith in the first, nevertheless scheme and strive against it with all sorts of devices, among them immigration exclusion acts, quotas, loyalty oaths, vows of allegiance, unpassable literacy tests. They shape barriers of nicknames: redneck, yank, mick, wop, frog, sheeny, yid, gook, chink, coon, nigger—all intended to stigmatize, to exclude and to deride difference. "Social" clubs do it in their way and college fraternities and sororities do it in theirs. The latter, within the larger academic community whose measure of belongingness is presumed to be scholarly excellence, abrogate this with invidious rules of selection, separating themselves as *soi-disant* "Greeks," from the unselect student majority whom they call barbs (short for barbarians). Among the barbs, they single out the Jews and Negroes for ultimate outsiders never to be inducted into their Greek fanes, ever to be excluded and derided beyond all the rest.

Altogether, it would seem that there is no reach of the culture where, late or soon, difference is not felt to be somehow a dangerous intrusion, a threat to its configuration, stirring the uneasiness, the anxiety, even the fear which are so much responses to its presence. Shutting it out, deriding it—especially while exploiting it—are reassuring antidotes that set up and nourish feelings of safety and superiority.

Now it happens that everywhere in the world, colors are used as signs and symbols for emotions, although which color for which emotion and in what order from glad to sad, varies within each culture and from culture to culture. Each develops its own not unambiguous pairing of status and mood with color; each ordains a color-scale more or less of its own to chart an order of esthetic preferences and moral values. Notoriously imprecise as are identifications of colors, clashes over the import of tints and hues are commonplace, within a color community and between such communities. We need only recall the divergent significances of *yellow* in "yellow streak," "yellow badge," "yellow robe"; of *red* in "red pope," "red robe," "red flag," "the reds." People appraise one another in terms of colors and color-scales, valuing men and women by their pigmentation, distinguishing them as members of white, yellow, red or black races.

Yet in point of fact no man alive has a white skin; at his lightest and healthiest his hue is pinkish-yellow and may vary to raw-red or to a brown so dark that unless he is otherwise identified as "white," he is classified as "black," "nigger" or, more genteelly, "colored man." "Color" is a status symbol, not a skin-pigment; usage in our land maintains "white" at the apex of an order of values. It signifies, according to occasion, the norm of force and form which Nietzsche symbolizes with his godless blond beast; others the manners and morals of medieval knighthood in flower, or the godly purity, integrity, kindness, propriety, justice, praised by the common Christian man: "he's a *white* man," "he treated me *white*," *white* magic, *white* Jew. Conversely, *white* signifies values diminishing downward, like the *white* lie, the *whitewash*, the *white* feather, lily-liver, to the pallor of panic and the lividness of death.[4]

"Black" figures similarly on a scale of appraisals. In point of fact, no man alive has a black skin; the darkest complexion both holds and reflects light. Seeing a deeply colored face simply, as it meets the eye, is an esthetic and moral experience no less positive than any that "white" signifies: it is such for the young white

---

[4] Among many African peoples, the *rites du passage*, with which the end of childhood and the coming of manhood are signalized, require that the body of the initiate be painted white. In their cultures, *white* is the color of death. For example, the Paugwe of West Africa expose their confirmants to the stings of particularly nasty ants and of the hairs on blister-raising pods of certain plants and shout, "We kill you." Once the rites are completed, the bodies of the now twice-born are painted red. *Red* signalizes the resurrection and the new life of the dead *white*.

child and the man of art. Like "white," "black" is the terminal of all achromatic sequences. The pigmentation of no human being attains either achromatic terminal; both are ever beyond, and all mankind are colored men, with complexions between "white" and "black" in some commingling of both. Usage, however, tends to keep "black" a symbol for all sorts of qualities we all would rather blackball—the foul, the dirty, the disgusting, the villainous, the idiotic, the cruel and immoral—the philosophically evil; it keeps current phrases such as *black* heart, *black* hand, *black* flag, *black* magic, *black* Friday, *black* Pope, *black* mood, *black* fate. Qualify a human being as in any way black, then, however vaguely, however heedlessly or kindly you mean this attribution (as is the wont and use of usage), you willy-nilly do him a wrong, now and again a monstrous, a cruelly tragic wrong. It is a wrong, however good your will, however humane and scientific your intentions. You know it even unknowing, and to condone the guilt you feel not knowing why, to quiet your conscience, you rationalize the stigma by treating its victim as deserving whatever degree of blackness you are yourself capable of. You don't have to be a "white" Southerner or Northerner of the United States. Although Verwoert Boers and Arab slavers may be exempt from such feelings, the Frenchman, the Belgian, the Briton, the Spaniard, the Dutchman, the Portuguese or any other western man in Africa is not.

Only, most "white" men in Africa are not Africans, while the "black" men in the United States are Americans, with an ancestry more ancient than that of the "white" Daughters of the American Revolution. The least awake among these Americans has some inkling of the American Idea. The most overtly submissive lives in an unvoiced resentment which sometimes gets roused to action by the hope which the Idea stirs even when he thinks it a lie; while the most aware and articulate such American breaks out like James Baldwin: "To be a Negro in this country and to be relatively conscious is to be in a rage all the time." The rage has two occasions: one, the "white" man's power and his self-proclaimed superiority; the other, the "black" man's blackness and the gratuitous penalties it lays upon him as "black" in the white world. To be free from these injustices, to be free, on equal terms, to emulate the white man in the entire economy of the culture, and to shape his own personal history like the white among whites, is his unalienable right. Whatever his pigmentation, he wants to "pass" in every way, on every level, that he can. He wants to pass, and to surpass; he wants to excel. How, then, can he not protest, with the lovely, talented Diana Sands: "Look at *me*, never mind my color?" How can he fail to confirm the observation of that perceptive psychologist, Kenneth Clark, that somehow, whites are the tacit Joneses of the "Dark Ghetto," even its little children often preferring white dolls? That he, himself, having entered the society of his white peers—personal, professional, political, humanitarian—feels as if he had been guilty of desertion, betrayed his own people?

Or he could see himself and his position from the point of view which that tragic man of genius, Richard Wright, disclosed so poignantly in his novel, *The Outsider:* that somehow today's Negro is both inside and outside the white man's culture; that "the problem really starts once the Negro gets his so-called rights. Is he going to be able to settle down and live the normal day to day life of the average American or will he still have his sense of outsideness?" Or he might endeavor to free himself from this sense of outsideness and his resentment of it by means of a program of self-segregation in the United States, Mississippi for choice, and with a choice of Arab names, Elijah Muhammad, Muhammad Ali (for Cassius Clay), and so on. There is something to think about in the event that Black Muslim hatred of their "white Anglo-Saxon Protestant" cultural milieu turns them, for neither religious rebirth nor proper renaming, to the dark pagan peoples of Africa but to the Near Eastern "white," Moslem Arabs, among whom many are still slave-holders and slave-traders. Negritude, with all it may intend regarding African works and ways, Africans arts, seems not to count for much in what the alienated American Negro would be moving toward.

The advocates of Negritude write almost entirely in French; their own self-alienation seems deeper than that of our American Wrights and Baldwins, and in the utterance of Frantz Fanon it moves outside the outsideness of even Richard Wright. Fanon, one of whose fans is J. P. Sartre, comes from Martinique. He is an acculturated Frenchman, by profession a psychiatrist. He rejects racism, is skeptical of the loyalty of African leaders to the liberation and well-being of their obviously still unable peoples. He addresses the leaders of both the free and the unfree nations. A plague on both your houses, he tells them. You have nothing for us darker-skinned peoples. We must needs start afresh as we are, from where we are, to learn and to make entirely our own the knowledges and the skills which give the pale-faces their power, and so establish ourselves as a Third World giving man's history a new direction. As for myself—so he cries, in *Peau Noir, Masques Blancs* (Black Skin, White Masks) of which the very title scorns the self-alienation its author suffers from—as for myself, I am as I am, equally right and free. If the white contests my humanity, I will show him, by bringing to bear on life all my weight as a man.[5]

To "show him" could well be one implication of the American Idea.

But neither the American white nor the American Negro realizes the American Idea in such Thoreau-like self-acquiescence and self-assertion. The proposition that all men are equal and can show it if they get the chance to do so, translates the labors of equalization into a wishful struggle for identification, and a pretense that the different are really already the same. What else, indeed, could *equal* justice under law mean, except indifference to differences, except ignoring differences and conducting court and police work as if differences did not exist? Since, however, they do exist, Americans must shut their eyes to them; seeing, they

---

[5] At a coffee house opening in Harlem, New York, with the help of a Federal loan, a Negro monologist declared: "I am proud of being black. Negroes are learning that the black man has a rich history, and are beginning to see that being black is no longer a stigma of shame and disgrace but a badge of honor. The sooner Negroes learn about themselves and their history, the better they will be able to cope with the white world" (New York *Times*, Nov. 15, 1965). The attitude is not unlike Frantz Fanon's, with the differences contributed by the situation to which it is a response. Of the latter, the Negro comedian Godfrey Cambridge once said to his mostly white listeners: "Let's face it, you're not going back to Europe and I'm not going back to Africa. We have too much going for us here. . . . I'm part of America and want to feel the whole world my kin. I just want to be a man. Life is a joy. I dig it."

must pretend not to see; recognizing, they must deny that there is anything to recognize; so far as the difference they perceive is a difference of color, they must be *color-blind*. The "colored man" must, as such, be the invisible man. Let the law and the courts see to it; justice is not sufficiently blind, if it be not also color-blind.

Nothing could be more fair-minded and well-meant than this metaphor. So far as I know, it was first used in 1896, by Mr. Justice Harlan, whose grandson of the same name is today, like his grandfather, an associate justice of our Supreme Court. The dissent in which the older Harlan used it was one of the most pregnant of his many, lonely dissents. It challenged the majority ruling in the case of Ferguson vs. Plessy: that the Jim Crow regulations of Southern railroads do not violate the Constitution. "The Constitution of the United States," Justice Harlan declared, "is color-blind."

The idea, "color-blind," caught on. It got repeated, with diversified phrasings, now and again, whenever the principle of the equality of the different is invoked. Not so long ago the President of the United States used it in a World's Fair address to the Jubilee Convention of the Amalgamated Clothing Workers of America. "I would remind you," he told the needle-trades workers and their guests, "that this is the centennial year, this is the hundredth anniversary of Abraham Lincoln's freeing the slaves of their chains—but he did not free America of her bigotry, nor did he free the Negro of his color. And *until education is unaware of race, until employment is blind to color* [the italics are mine] *emancipation may be a proclamation but it is not a fact*."

And if the operative condition be what Mr. Johnson's language took it for, emancipation will always be a proclamation, never a fact. To embody proclamation in fact calls for awareness of race, seeing of color; for accepting, respecting, appreciating and working with them *as* they are *where* they are. For morally, color is a fact, a global fact; color is *the* fact, the vital decisive fact, the actually and potentially creative fact, and today's Great Divide for any future mankind may propose for themselves. Refusing to see this, to recognize it as it is for what it is, but deepens the predicament into which the hope of alienating the unalienable sinks alike the aggressors and the resisters among Americans, whether light-complexioned or darker. Not alone for them, but for all the peoples of the world, the metaphor "color-blind" brings an ominous self-deception. It would found a moral and cultural necessity by analogy with a physiological defect and a psychological lack. Its implications contravene the intent of the American Idea and of the Constitution that is to keep realizing it, which they invoke to confirm the Idea. Idea and Constitution postulate precisely that ungrudging acceptance of "color" in all its relations which blindness would shut off; they postulate equality in rights and freedoms for the differents *as* differents. To bring to bear a different metaphor, they postulate the self-commensuration of incommensurables. There is an old essay of William James's which he entitled *On a Certain Blindness in Human Beings.* Among the many defects to which this essay is an antidote is the color-blindness that John Harlan, in the cause of justice, endows the Constitution with. James's insight renews and advances the American Idea. It might make nutritious reading for all engaged in the struggles over alienating the unalienable.

4 | The American Dream and
the American Idea:
A Predicament of the
Pragmatic Intelligence

I

The American Dream!

This phrase is the inspiration of James Truslow Adams, who in the thirty-fourth year of his life abandoned a career of business for one of public service and this, when at last the First World War came to its uneasy stoppage in a series of "peace" treaties, for a career of historian of our own United States. A man of heart as well as learning, Adams was deeply concerned with the meaning of American works and ways for the commonality of mankind. All his studies seem to focus on this relationship between the people of the United States and between this country and the rest of the world. The book which signalizes its meaning as "the American Dream" was his *Epic of America*, published in 1931. It had been prepared, composed, and printed while the "prosperity" of the Hoover era was teetering into the Great Depression; its greatest vogue came with the New Deal; it spread southward to Latin America, across the Atlantic to Italy, to Poland, to Germany, to Hungary, to France, to Denmark, to Spain—mostly lands becoming fearful of freedom and skeptical of democracy; but also lands whose peoples were bound by blood and benefits to sons and daughters, brothers and sisters, husbands and fathers, or simply to fellow villagers who had adventured to that "golden land," America, to seek a life and a living that should satisfy. *The Epic of America* was translated into all their tongues; it proffered them the glad tidings of "the American Dream." James Adams wrote in the preface to his *Epic:*

> That American Dream of a better, richer, happier life for all citizens of every rank, which is the greatest contribution we have yet made to the thought and welfare of the world. That dream or hope had been present from the start, ever since we became an independent nation. Each generation has seen an uprising of the ordinary Americans to save the dream from the forces which appear to be overwhelming and dispelling it. Possibly the greatest of these struggles lies just ahead of us, at the present time: not a struggle of revolutionists against the established order, but of the ordinary men to hold fast to those rights to life, liberty and the pursuit of happiness which were vouchsafed to us in the past, in vision and on parchment.

But Adams does not see the struggle as a consequence of commitment to these rights, declared "on parchment" to be "unalienable." He sees it rather, as he tells in the epilogue to his *Epic,* as a consequence of "the American dream, that dream of a land in which life should be better and richer and fuller for every man with opportunity for each according to his ability or achievement." Opportunity, he declared, must include culture as well as wealth, else the land may become the "Babbitt warren" it runs the danger of becoming. Opportunity means pushing to keep up with the Joneses, and the Joneses whom the dreamers of the American Dream should strive to overtake are the culturally as well as the economically "successful." Their symbolic house of life or temple should be neither a bank building nor the Capitol; it should be the Library of Congress.

It is in this sense of the American Dream that Dean Rusk

offered himself to the ministers of the American States meeting at Punta del Este in Uruguay, as an instance of the success stories which keep incarnating the Dream.

It is the story told again and again by Horatio Alger and Oliver Optic. In this story freedom figures not as the end but as a means[1]—"the most reliable means," the Secretary of State told his

[1] "Perhaps you would forgive me for a personal recollection. Like millions of present-day North Americans, I spent my earliest years in what people would now call underdeveloped circumstances. We were prescientific and pretechnical; we were without public health or medical care; typhoid, pellagra, hookworm, and malaria were a part of the environment in which Providence had placed us. Our schools were primitive. Our fathers and mothers earned a meager living with backbreaking toil.

"But the great adventure through which many of us have lived has seen the transformation of our lives in a short period—a transformation brought about by the magical combination of education, health, and increasing productivity. On our farms we felt the impact of the indispensable partnership among education, scientific research, and the extension of knowledge to those who could put it to practical use.

"Neighbor helped neighbor to build a house, a barn, to pass along the new methods. They joined together to build roads until public funds could take over the burden. They pooled their limited resources to hire a schoolteacher or a doctor. Bits of capital began to accumulate and this was reinvested in growth and development. More and more young people managed to get to the university, and more and more of these brought their learning back to the benefit of their own people.

"These changes did not take place without struggle. Years of thought and work and debate were required to prepare America for the necessary steps of self-help and social reform. I remember well the bitter resistance before Franklin Roosevelt was able to win support for the Tennessee Valley Authority, that immense network of dams and power which has wrought such miraculous changes in our South. But a succession of progressive leaders, determined to bring about social change within a framework of political consent, carried through an "alliance for progress" within the United States."

Lyndon Johnson, after his election to the Presidency, told of his own personal exemplification of the American Dream again and again, and he is but a more notable instance of a vast multitude who, affirming freedom, made or found opportunity to exercise it and to create means to nourish its growth, at least for themselves if not for all Americans. Theodore Roosevelt, Calvin Coolidge, and Herbert Hoover thus shared in it. Of course the segregation of the American Dream from the American Idea is a persistent endeavor, and this has been assimilated to "the Protestant Ethic." It has been noted in "Poor Richard's Almanac," in McGuffey's *Readers*, in Bruce Barton's reconstruction of the New Testament Jesus into a twentieth-century salesman, and in many others—from G. H. Lorimer's *Letters from a Self-Made Merchant to His Son*, to the ratiocinations of Dale Carnegie. That it has transatlantic predecessors and parallels, such as the *Letters* of the fourth Lord Chesterfield to his son, does not save the Dream from identification

audience, "to economic development and social justice." History shows, he said, "that the humane and pragmatic methods of free men are not merely the right way morally, to develop an under-developed country; they are technically the efficient way."

The Dream, as Adams himself interpreted it, was first a vision of life more abundant and again of saving certain unalienable rights from ever imminent alienation. The nature of these rights, the relation between them and life more abundant, are assumed and disclosed *ambulando*. The Dream figures as a creed and a code, as a faith to work and fight for which renders any true believer from anywhere an "ordinary American." The Dream is that substance of the things he hopes for, that evidence of the things he does not see whence come the direction and form of his struggle for survival. The Dream is that configuration of ends and means whose interplay shapes up into the Dreamer's selfhood, into the singularity of the Dreamer's personal history. Adams' *Epic of America* purports to tell how the people called Americans labored and fought to inform their ways and works with their vision of abundance and to enact vision into fact so as to invest their Dream with the reality of the waking life.

Perhaps this was the miracle of a God who works in mysterious ways his wonders to perform; perhaps it was the joke of the goddess Serendipity; perhaps the blind goodwill of the anarch Anomie—let philosophers of history argue the alternatives. Somehow, "American Dream" came to be used as a pat locution for every species of sentiment which the image of America evoked, abroad as at home. Usage rendered the phrase a global symbol with meanings as varied as the meaners. Mankind's struggles for survival going on as they do go on, the means they use are more conscious, more explicit, more visible than the ends which the means serve, nourish, or consummate in. The ends perdure, the means change with time, place, and occasion; they get altered as chance suggests or need discovers. Every variety of *Homo sapiens* attends first to the means for "life, liberty, and the pursuit of happiness," for these ends-in-themselves which are the substance

---

with a conscienceless "materialism." Nor does the present version of Dream and Idea modify the global slander of America that its Dream degrades end into means, making of Freedom a mere tool.

of survival. Success and failure thus signalize the role of means, and hence means become objects of "ultimate concern." Their functions get hypostatized: the tools of survival, be they grandfathers, gods, or golems, get exalted into its idols to be suicidally served and tended with a devotion which only things worshiped receive.

Perhaps this is why, although not solely why, the trend of usage has been to strip the American Dream of its prophet's essential intent, to segregate the means he recorded from the ends he affirmed, to divorce the stuffs, the tools, and the manners and morals of a "better, richer, and happier life" from the simpler urgencies which are the thrust of life as such. Within a decade, the American Dream became part of the American idiom with a global glossolalia. Now it is even being used in titles of bitter "absurd" stage plays and antinovels, in literary periodicals and collegiate debates, in party politics at home and ideological disputations abroad. The general tendency has become to treat the phrase as identifying liberty with subversive "un-Americanism" or massed anonymity; as identifying equality with conformity; and striving to excel with "bringing up father" and "keeping up with the Joneses." Nowadays American Dream identifies progress with the multiplication of tools and things and personal possessions; it identifies success with that bitch-goddess of William James' whose worship consists in ruthlessly accumulating pelf and power and in displaying them like a peacock his tail; it identifies satisfaction with self-deception or contrived illusion. And what are the identifications, if not mutations, of Emerson's mid-nineteenth-century American renewal of that global, ageless complaint that one's fellow countrymen are materialists and conformists; that "things are in the saddle and ride mankind"?

I have the impression that Thoreau is today the preferred spokesman of this age-old insight which assimilates individuality to liberty and liberty to disengagement from the possessions, the things, and the tools that, on the record, appear to possess their possessor and enslave their user, so making men such prisoners of their properties that they forfeit their selfhood as end to their preoccupation with its means. Mankind's authentic end is freedom, and as Tocqueville observed to his age, "the man who asks of freedom anything other than freedom is born to be a slave." Although within James Adams' telling of the American Dream, no man would be born to be a slave; the Dream would work to render him one.

II

To the abolitionists among the Dreamers, liberty was the fighting faith. They held liberty to be man's paramount end; they quoted chapter and verse to verify that government was created by the consent of the governed so that it might serve as a means and only a means "to secure [for all men equally] those rights" of "life, liberty, and the pursuit of happiness." They repudiated the spreading displacement of ends by means and exalted the ends in the measure that the powers whom they challenged exalted the means.

The representative voice of this creed and of the code which it energized was Theodore Parker, another member of the generation of Emerson, of Thoreau, of Tocqueville. His phrase for the configuration of ends and means that he believed Armericanism to signify was not the American Dream. It was the *American Idea*.

Emerson called Parker "our Savonarola." By vocation he was a minister of religion, although he said of himself that nature meant him to be a philosopher. Spokesmen for the people who lived a life only saddled and ridden by things denounced him as an agitator, a stump orator; and perhaps it would not have been altogether misleading to speak of him as a philosopher urging his philosophic faith from the stump. Like Emerson and Thoreau, Parker, an individualist and transcendentalist, instead of withdrawing from the workaday world into an esoteric nature sustaining her visible forms, put his faith to work among the men so ridden by things that they dehumanized other men into chattels to own and buy and sell. Parker grew up struggling for a livelihood and a life in the conviction that the American Declaration of Independence, which set forth what he signalized as the *American Idea*, was no pretense; that as a definition of ends and means it meant what it said. The American Idea was no dream to him; it was the reality of the working, fighting faith on which he bet his life. A poor boy making his way among the farmers and store-keepers of Lexington, Massachusetts, he grew up in a climate of remembrance of a war for freedom and independence the scars of which were still green when Great Britain imposed a second war on her former colonies; many of the heroes of the first war were still alive: Adams and Jefferson and Madison and others who had helped define for the new nation the freedom and independence which Parker labored and studied to achieve for himself in his own personal history. Although a student who worked his way through Harvard College with the ministry for his chosen calling, Parker was as much a self-taught as a self-made man, winning his way to notable leadership in the Unitarian church and the abolitionist movement—not one of Oliver Optic's models of "success." Parker's career was brief; he was only fifty when he died. He did realize the American Dream as Adams was later to envision it; he did successfully realize it. But he also realized the American Idea, as he himself signalized it, and he heroically vindicated both. In his life each, Dream and Idea, so reinforced the other that each was practically disclosed and verified by its relation to the other. The relation is such that the Dream, when it is segregated from the Idea, ceases to be authentically American.

What, then, is the American Idea?

Parker rang out the phrase, so far as I know, for the first time in the nation's history, on the twenty-ninth of May, 1850. The place was Boston's Faneuil Hall, the occasion a mass meeting to denounce the fugitive slave law. Parker was called from that meeting to help save an escaping slave from being returned to his lawful owner in the law-abiding South. Before he was called away Parker made his speech. He told his audience:

> There is what I call the American Idea. I so name it because it seems to me to lie at the basis of all our truly original distinctive and American institutions. It is itself a complex idea, composed of three subordinate and more simple ideas, namely, the idea that all men have unalienable rights, that in respect thereof, all men are created equal, and that government is to be established and sustained, for the purpose of giving every man an opportunity for the enjoyment and development of all these unalienable rights. This idea demands that the proximate organization thereof be a democ-

racy, that is, a government of all the people, by all the people, for all the people; of course, a government after the principles of eternal justice, the unchanging law of God. For shortness' sake, I will call it the idea of freedom. That is one idea.

And the other is, that one man has a right to hold another man in thralldom, not for the slave's good, but for the master's convenience; not on account of any wrong the slave had done, or intended, but solely for the benefit of the master. This idea is not peculiarly American. For shortness' sake, I shall call it the idea of slavery. It demands for its proximate organization, an aristocracy, that is, a government of all the people by a part of the people, the master, for a part of the people, the masters, against the part of the people, the slaves; a government contrary to the principles of eternal justice, contrary to the unchanging law of God.

These two ideas are hostile, irreconcilably hostile, and can no more be compromised and made to coalesce in the life of this nation than the worship of the real God, and the worship of the imaginary Devil can be combined and made to coalesce in the life of a single man. An attempt has been made to reconcile and unite the two. The slavery clause of the Constitution of the United States is one monument to this attempt. The results of this attempt, you see what they are; not order but confusion. And as you know, they continue to be had.

The "idea of freedom" signalizing man as the end; "the idea of slavery" signalizing man as a means; and man's history a struggle between those seeking to reduce other men to means and to keep them thus, and those striving to so diversify and so order means as to assure to all men their equality as ends! The soldiers of freedom pursue the liberation of the human person through the instrumentality of his insights, of his inventions, and of the goods and services which those produce. They call upon no Hegelian dialectic, nor any para-Aristotelian or Teilhardian sequential hierarchy; they assume an alpha perhaps, but no omega. What they signalize is the Idea of Freedom. They hold it to be the dynamic of mankind's struggle, diverse generation upon diverse generation, to live on and grow; the dynamic of mankind's propelling themselves, making themselves over by means of their lore, their learning, their inventions, and their acceptances and rejections of the uses of them in the successive actualizations of their changing dreams.

Together these doings make up the history of culture as the

humanization of the earth. Mankind's cultures, be they eolithic or post-modern, are mankind's means: they are the ways and works by which peoples survive or fail to—but they are not the survival. The survival is the unresting urge, the unyielding élan in the process of their succession. It is the flow of energy which creates and sustains the cultures that inform and alter it. Immemorial tradition names this élan "spirit," and it is as spirit, by spirit, and for spirit that the generations outlive the cultures they are born into, passing beyond them or receding away from them into other, more satisfying ones. Generations may also be arrested in their cultures so that the struggle to live on becomes a present repetition of a past with no future, thus with neither a personal nor an interpersonal history. And this is the plight of any individual or society when the makings ride their makers; the latter then become the slaves and idolaters of the producings and products of their arts, their sciences, their religions, their political or cultural economies. Their Dream, enfleshed, has ceased to draw its energy and shape from the Idea of Freedom; they enflesh it, insisting that it is the Idea which sucks both energy and shape from the Dream.

Yet the record attests that it is the Idea which the unenslaved and the enslaved alike take for granted. Aware or not, the members of each of the diverse and divergent families of human culture feel, singly and together, that freedom to live on, and to pursue, by whatever means, the ends which consummate for them as "happiness," is their unalienable right; they feel that all their economies, both the natural and the supernatural, are first and last means "to secure those rights," and they revere them like idols because of their role as means. Singly, hence, mankind strive with one another; jointly, they war with one another over owning and using means. The rivalries obtain in every region of the human enterprise: recall Albert Einstein's ironic observation while he was still a member of the Kaiser Wilhelm Institut in pre-Nazi Berlin: "If my theory works, the French will call me a Jew and the Germans will call me a German; if it fails, the French will call me a German, while the Germans will call me a Jew." Recall also that his theory did work and the Hitler Germans called him a Jew and denounced his theory; so, likewise, did the Stalin Russians. And now set beside these enlightening rivalries first the fact that

Einstein was both the grandfather and the prophet of the atom bomb and that he was committed with a devout, undeviating commitment to the ideas of equal liberty and universal peace; and beside this set the fact that these are ends which the Universal Declaration of Human Rights details, over the signature of practically all mankind's official representatives, as the joint and several goals of them all.

III

The *Idea of Freedom*, that which Theodore Parker had signalized as the *American Idea*, is, in the Universal Declaration, primary and seminal. The Declaration starts from mankind as they are, to challenge and change what they are. It takes for granted that they are countless and ever multiplying multitudes of human individuals, each somehow different from all others and living together with some others in diverse places, by diverse means, in diverse ways. It postulates that this difference, this singularity of the person, is *the* unalienable right, the equal of every other such everywhere in the world. It postulates that associations of the differents with one another make up unions conceived, covenanted, and implemented in order that each—be it a person, a people, a state, a church, or any other corporation or establishment—may live on more freely, more abundantly, more creatively and safely, than it could by struggling on alone.

Some take these postulates for articles of faith as otherworldly and as irrelevant to this world as any that *Homo sapiens* ever purported to bet his survival on. Others take them for working hypotheses, the fruit of diverse mankind's historical experiences, of which both the American Dream and its not too ambiguous realizations are one visible verification; a verification so visible, at least with respect to the means, as to be envied and emulated by all, and by foes even more vigorously than by friends. The foes, dreaming the Dream independently of the Idea, merely shape up some variant of Parker's "idea of slavery," some somnambulant totalitarianism which becomes in due course as destructive of itself as it is from its beginning aggressive against what differs from itself. May we not so read the histories of genu-

inely would-be totalitarian societies past and present? Of the sacerdotal, the Communist, the Fascist, the Nazi, or any combination
of them? It is incidental that they call themselves "peoples' democracies," "guided democracies," or otherwise freedomless democracies; their naming is but the respect that perforce tyranny
pays to liberty. It is incidental that they arrange enclaves of selected liberties such as the Soviets provide for their scientists.[2]
Those liberties are pseudo-liberties: they are the liberties of the
slave to do the bidding of his master duly and in good order—or
else. They are instruments of imperialist policy, not of advance-
ments of knowledge and of its free exchange with the rest of the
world. They are not freedom to grow in freedom by the exercise

[2] From 1921 to 1934, Piotr L. Kapitza, now long head of the Institute of Physics Problems in Soviet Moscow, had been an associate of Lord Rutherford at
the Cavendish Laboratory of England's Cambridge University. In 1934, he
paid a visit to Stalin-bound Russia. Prevented from returning to England,
he devoted himself to his set scientific tasks, with resigned courage and variable fortunes, whose ups and downs at last brought his appointment to the
headship of this institute. In 1966, after nearly a quarter of a century, it became possible for him to return to England on a visit and to pay his tribute
to Lord Rutherford, the man and the scientist. In the issue of August 12,
1966, *Science* published a report on "Kapitza's Visit to England" by Victor
K. McElheny. The report ends with a quotation from Kapitza's lecture on
Rutherford. "The year that Rutherford died (1938) there disappeared forever the happy days of free scientific work which gave us such delight in
our youth. Science has lost her freedom. Science has become a productive
force. She has become rich but she has become enslaved and part of her is
veiled in secrecy. I do not know whether Rutherford would continue nowadays to joke and laugh as he used to do."
    "Since 1961," Harvard's J. M. H. Lindbeck wrote in the New York
Times of January 8, 1967, "China's leaders have tried to protect scientists and
engineers from the unsettling effects of the regime's political programs. The
group is the only one exempt, for example, from full engulfment in the current political indoctrination campaign. This was provided for in the sixteen-
point charter for the Great Proletarian Cultural Revolution issued by the
Central Committee of the Chinese Communist party last Aug. 8: 'As regards
scientists, technicians and ordinary members of working staffs, as long as
they are patriotic, work energetically, are not against the party and Socialism, and maintain no illicit relations with any foreign country, we should in
the present movement continue to apply the policy of unity, criticism, duty
(i.e., changing scientists' views via small-group discussions rather than by
more coercive means). Special care should be taken of those scientists and
scientific and technical personnel who have made contributions. Efforts
should be made to help them gradually transform their world outlook and
their style of work.'"

of freedom. They are privileges, permissions such as dairy cattle have, which their owner feeds and shelters and breeds for his personal profit, not the animals' well-being and free growth into the excellence natural to their kind. They are but the owner's means, to be abolished if they fail to serve the owner's ends.

Confusions of privilege with unalienable right, confusion of the permitted with the authentic, of changeable and changing means with perduring ends—in sum, of Dream with Idea—are universal and endemic: the confusions occur in any formation of interpersonal relationships, on any scale. Robert Michels, studying the structure and function of political parties, declared that it was "a fundamental sociological law" for such parties—and all organizations, notably the revolutionary—to become oligarchies; that is, to seek to crowd out liberty with authority, to subdue the unalienable rights of the many into the means of power of a few, and all as phases of a struggle "to secure those rights." So in our United States, North and South. Nine years after Theodore Parker signalized the menace of the confusion with that speech in Faneuil Hall, Abraham Lincoln told the American people: "The principles of Jefferson are the definitions and axioms of free society, and yet are denied and evaded with no small success. One dashingly calls them 'glittering generalities.' Another bluntly calls them 'self-evident lies' and others invidiously argue that they apply to 'superior races.' These expressions are the vanguard, the miners and sappers of returning despotism." And four years later, at Gettysburg, he told the world that "the great Civil War" which Americans were then engaged in was testing whether *any* nation conceived in liberty and dedicated to the proposition that all men are created equal could long endure—testing, that is, the realism and practicality of the American Idea.

Debunkers to the contrary notwithstanding, the champions and defenders of the Idea won the war and forthwith submerged the end in an imagining, devising, and employing of means (the course of events is today scorned as "the gilded age"). They not only took from dark-skinned Americans the equal liberty which their country's Constitution now guaranteed them, but they also drew multitudes from all the peoples of Europe and Asia to join to the native Negro, and demand of all of them that they should

believe, obey, and serve the Dream as their new employers interpreted it to them.

Only the newcomers would not. On the whole and in the
long run, Truslow Adams reminds us, they did not. Together
with the "native" heirs of the faith of the Parkers and the Lin-
colns, they advanced their own interpretation of the American
Dream, and in this interpretation the role of the American Idea
continued paramount. In every region of the nation's economy
they began as pioneers and ended as heroes of the "uprisings"
which Adams' *Epic* recounts—"ordinary Americans" rising up
"to serve the dream," and "to hold fast to those [unalienable]
rights" of theirs against every scheme and stratagem of alienation.
Without knowing it, they kept betting their lives as Thoreau had
bet his: "If one advances confidently in the direction of his
dreams, and endeavours to lead the life which he imagines, he will
meet with a success unimagined in the common hours. . . . If
you have built castles in the air, your work need not be lost, that
is where they should be. Now put the foundations under them."
Indeed, what would have been the sequences from Benjamin
Franklin and natural science à la Newton to the Atomic Energy
and other Commissions and natural science à la Einstein and his
posterity? From steam engines to cybernetics and automation?
From horse and buggy on earth to rockets to the moon? From
muzzle-loading muskets to electronic missiles and atom bombs?
From business cycles to "the affluent society"? And concurrently
from country town to megalopolis and from "little red school-
house" to "higher education" for everybody? What would have
been the sequence, I ask, without the will and vision of "the ordinary American" *freely* taking the ineluctable risks of putting
foundations under his castles in the air?

IV

The global import of intent and commitment which postulated the American Idea is already suggested in eighty-year-old
Benjamin Franklin's letter to a friend in England after his country's Constitutional Convention:

I send enclos'd the propos'd new Federal Constitution for these States. I was engag'd four months of the last summer in the Convention that form'd it. It is now sent by Congress to the several States for their confirmation. If it succeeds, I do not see why you might not in Europe carry the Project of good Henry the Fourth into Execution, by forming a Federal Union and One Grand Republic of all its different States and kingdoms; by means of a like Convention; for we had many interests to reconcile.

In the light of the American Idea, this Federal Constitution was a means whereby the end of equal liberty for the diverse might advance and maintain itself. By no means a perfect means, it had to be improved by amendments whose declared functions were in turn perverted by prostituting them, in the name of equal liberty, to privilege subversive of equal liberty. The struggle for and against this ongoing transvaluation of means into ends is waged by voluntary associations of Americans in many formations of which the political party is simply one. The Epic of America spans the ups and downs of trades unions, of professional guilds, of religious and antireligious societies, of ethnic, racial, and racist groupings, of military, "patriotic," and "revolutionary" organizations, of configurations of interest from all the disciplines of industry, the sciences, the arts, and the crafts, and of their economies. Not the least among them are peace societies with their divergent creeds—from a refusal to bear arms to a demand that arms shall be borne only to enforce peace.

But the shouting and the tumult of these multitudes ever and again become the chorus of "the ordinary man," vindicating the American Idea and retooling the American Dream. The Idea of Freedom was the creative urge toward the lesser American ends of the First World War; it gave its spirit to Woodrow Wilson's dream of the Fourteen Points, with their program of self-determination of the peoples, with their project of a League of Nations "to make the world safe for democracy." The Idea of Freedom was the working hypothesis of the New Deal; it animated Franklin Roosevelt's vision of the *terminus ad quem* of the Second World War, with his specification of "the Four Freedoms" and of the new media of their incarnation at home. The Idea became an all-world projection as the charter of the United Nations, as the Universal Declaration of Human Rights and as the global organization's agencies intending for all mankind what Benjamin Franklin had thought the peoples of Europe might seek for themselves and now seem to. Regardless of what American aficionados of special interests or spokesmen for political parties might continue to argue about the "national purpose" and the "national goals," the immediate ones—the "ends-in-view," as John Dewey called them—come and pass. Those are but items of the Dream, but successions of means which, among all men everywhere, the perduring end of liberty, growing and diversifying, shapes and reshapes, according to their plight of need and desire, frustration and arrest—the liberty which is life not merely as it uses its means but uses them up and creates new ones in its ongoing self-diversification.

As history measures time the interval is brief yet the way long from George Washington's warning against "entangling alliances" to John Kennedy's declaration that the nation's service to the peoples of the world, as they realize that certain of their rights are unalienable, is "to make the world safe for diversity" by helping the families of man wherever they dream to win "a better, richer, happier life" and wherever they exercise these rights in order to turn Dream into reality. Making the world safe for diversity, vindicating all men's equal right to be their different selves without penalty and without privilege, in the face of wars hot and wars cold waged to alienate this right, has somehow, unplanned step by step, brought the peace-craving American people to create arms more powerful and more plentiful than any in the world; it has projected soldiering into an organic function of citizenship; it has stationed American troops in more than thirty lands; it has committed the nation to defending the freedom and independence of forty-two and to supplying one hundred or more with arms, money, tools, food, medicines, and other goods and services, yet never enough; it has sent the men and women (and never enough of them) of all ages and conditions who freely joined its Peace Corps to teach, as comprehensively as their pupils are able to learn, the knowledge and the know-how whereby America has been rendered the mighty and generous Jones of twentieth-century mankind—the Jones at the same time envied, feared, ridiculed, abused, and exploited for gifts of goods and services. To teach so that these new dreamers might, by learning, free their own powers to create for themselves the "better, richer, happier life" they dream of.

In addition, the American taxpayer, out of the abundance of his Dream embodied in the waking life of his expanding economy of abundance, contributes to the support of the vital functions of the United Nations a more than proportionate share of their costs. Those functions are not the suppression of conflict or the enforcement of "peace." They are the functions of UNO agencies and councils better known by their initials than their official designations—ECOSOC, UNESCO, ECAPE, ILO, FAO, GATT, IDA, IFC, IMF, and the like. Aware or unaware, the economic philosophy of our "affluent society" has in view Maynard Keynes' warning regarding the economic consequences of the "peace" negotiated after World War I; and it designs, so far successfully, that the like shall not recur. In the substantial endeavors to make real the Dream which is the Charter of the United Nations, it has not. Yet the current secretary-general of this global confederation of states old and new, societies free and bond, mighty and mightless, is at pains to declare that in view of the insecure starved lives which most of mankind live, "To preach . . . the virtues of democracy is not only irrelevant but comic. . . . The remedy is to do away with the causes of illiteracy, disease and poverty . . . we have to go to the root of the problem if we are to establish a stable world order, if we are to see the principles of the United Nations Charter implemented in all parts of the world."

But it is the honorable gentleman, his paternalist and schoolmasterly mind ignoring the very vocal preachments of the virtues of authoritarian totalitarianism in its Communist form, who is here, if not Tartuffian, like Dostoevsky's Grand Inquisitor, comic and irrelevant. He must know well that illiteracy, disease, and poverty prevail in the lands where democracy is not preached and its opposite is practiced. He must well know how old is the story that the dream of a world without illiteracy, disease, and poverty cannot be made real without the free commitment, the will and work, of the sick, the hungry, and the ignorant to make it real. It cannot be done *for* them, by grace of authority, even of a loving

Heavenly Father. It can only be done *with* them and *by* them, in freedom, for freedom; and unless they first determine and strive, jointly and severally, to learn how to live on as good neighbors responsible for themselves, to themselves, and to one another, no gifts, no counsel, no coercion will move their wills to serve their needs or diversify their wants. To render them aware that the Idea of Freedom is each living man's unalienable end, to persuade them to seek together the understanding and the skills wherewith the Dream of abundance and security is transposed from Dream into reality, is a preachment which teaches "the virtues of democracy." It directs men's wills with the imagination of "ends-in-view" and of the means thereto which, whatever the fields of their endeavor be, transmutes Dream from a consoling sedative or an envious irritant into a creative program for the ongoing expansion of their freedom.

How much of this has been achieved by the agencies of the United Nations, by free transnational unions of diverse interests, and by voluntary associations of "private" citizens, is hardly guessed. The record has been buried under accounts of the cold and intermittently hot wars and of the rude and malicious disputations of totalitarians against democrats which are the talking aspects of these wars. The shootings and the talkings are both highly audible, highly visible, and highly evocative of a manifold of conflicting reverberations among the peoples of the pluralistic democracies. They are all news, and exciting. The laborious, slow, not quickly noticeable progress of *aggiornamento*, of updating in the diverse economies of mankind, is neither. But short of a war of annihilation, the power of survival is in the latter, not the former. And the signal instance of this power, which in our postmodern culture of electronics, computers, and self-realizing science fiction has become unmistakably visible around the globe, is the reconstruction of the American Dream by the American Idea again resurgent in the United States.

The resurgence began somewhat more than a decade ago, with a unanimous decision of the American Supreme Court specifically affecting Negroes in the nation's schools, but consequential for all the other ways and works of the nation's life. The decision made it clear that the formula "separate but equal" of an earlier decision would because they are different is to penalize some and to privilege others; that the formula "separate but equal" of an earlier descision would alienate, from both of the separated, that unalienable right of equal liberty which it is the function of the Constitution to keep secure. At an earlier time a well-meaning justice of the Supreme Court had implied the same thing by declaring that the Constitution is "color-blind," heedless of the fact that colorblindness is a dangerous physical defect; that as a metaphor applied to the relations between persons of different skin color, it could be a moral defect, since it calls for ignoring what the persons actually are and pretending they are not what they are. Only when every Negro—and yes, every non-Negro no less —can take for granted that he may live and move and achieve his appropriate excellence among his non-Negro and Negro fellow Americans, that he may freely and safely *as* Negro, *as* non-Negro, exercise and perfect his own powers at his own risk, without privilege and without penalty, only then is his equal liberty secure in fact as in law. The same holds, of course, for all human individuals, since each one's identity consists, as it must, of the singular configuration of properties which together compose his individuality; since each person's survival and growth are his ineffably unalienable right as the American Idea affirms this right and as the American Dream would effectuate it.

During the more than a decade just passed, the least favored of "ordinary Americans" have been "uprising" to hold fast to those rights which the American Idea signifies, and by its inspiration to save their American Dream from the forces (new and old) which "appear to be overwhelming and dispelling it." Their uprising figures but as part of a greater one, national in its "end-in-view," international in its sweep. Today, its protean Dream of means happens to be renamed "The Great Society," but save for the thrust of the Idea of Freedom, the Dream stays a figment of the wishful imagination. That thrust is the thrust of life struggling to live on. Thomas Jefferson wrote it thus in 1774: "The God who gave us life gave us liberty at the same time; the hand of force may destroy but cannot disjoin them."

V

As Truslow Adams conceived it, and as the record establishes it, Everyman's Dream of "a better, richer, happier life" is one thing; its actualization in the tools, the techniques, the goods, and the services of any "American way of life" is another. By means of those the non-Joneses of our United States bring themselves to parity with the Joneses they struggle to keep up with. Replacing scarcity by abundance, poverty by affluence, they come into the security and certainty which put an end to their quest. They have "made good"; they are "successes." The "better, richer, happier life" wherewith the Dream came true is now aspiration exhausted in possession, years of labor ended in a longer Sabbath of leisure, existence precipitated from ongoing diversification into, at most, a cumulative repetition of identicals. As the Dream comes true, Freedom gets contained or suppressed; creating values ends up in duplicating and conserving them; living on becomes conspicuous as a stasis of consumption which, ironically enough, arouses the moralists still aspiring at home and the envious and emulative souls hungering abroad to denounce the Dreamer of the American Dream as a materialist composition of greeds and lusts which assume his possessions into idols whose empty providence he trusts and worships.

Their judgments are as false as their motives are natural. They but display the judges more reliably than they account for what they condemn. As Jefferson believed, the providential thing is—those who *see* not providence but chance might prefer to say, "the lucky thing is"—that life and liberty *are* inseparable and survive or perish together. Hence, the American Dream, wherever it comes true, comes true under the pervading strains and stresses from the American Idea, strains and stresses which compound as they mount, until freedom overcomes security and certainty, conserving gives way again to creating, and the Dream is liquidated by the Idea.

I have come to believe that the predicament of the pragmatic intelligence is the same as this relationship between Dream and Idea. I see it in the meanings which conventional usage gives the word "pragmatic" and its cognates. I see it in the ratiocinative order which usage signalizes as "intelligence" and its cognates. The former petrifies production—of skills no less than commodities—in product; the latter translates diversifying functions into repetitions of identicals—into the disclosure of some same which, true believers assert, grounds the diversifications always and everywhere. I believe that authentic pragmatists—yes, I recognize that "authentic" is invidious—do not thus understand "pragmatic intelligence"; that they might take "pragmatic" as synonymous with "creative," and by the phrase signify workings out of the perception that the thoughts which humans think are events of the struggles in which they live on and grow, and that the values which the thinkers assign them—for example, truth, goodness, rightness, loveliness—are first and last survival values which thoughts gain or lose as their felt role in the thinkers' struggle serves it or foils it. I believe, too, that authentic pragmatists tend to take that multimeaninged word "intelligence" as they take "pragmatic." They follow its historic transvaluations from its Latin beginning as *inter legere* (i.e., a bringing together and choosing from an assembled diversity those items that might be fitted to one another in order to strengthen the fitter's struggle to survive) into some one ultimate set of "first principles" that, by demoting the flow and freedom of actual experience from reality into appearance, shall guarantee the believer security and certainty forever.

Since such guarantees are ineffables, their invariancy is asserted to enclose all variation. "Pragmatic intelligence" finds itself in the Sisyphean predicament of both doing its stuff over and over again within this metaphysical enclosure and striving to go free. Soon or late, like the pioneer of the American frontier, it does break away from the settlement into the wilderness. The tension between the American Dream and the American Idea signalizes the condition. For the survival of any "American Way," the Idea must needs impel the Dreamer to the day he dies, out of the settlement of his Dream toward the wilderness beyond. Our experience, aware and unaware, of transvaluing our Dream from a house of safety and certainty into a walled prison, and of thrusting out as thinkers and doers over open spaces toward other places, often consummates in a fluency which we denote by the word "freedom," unmodified. William James speaks of this experience of fluency as a "sort of anaesthic state in which we might say with Walt Whitman, 'I am sufficient as I am.' " He describes it as a "feeling of the sufficiency of the present moment, of its absoluteness, an absence of all need to explain it, to account for it, to 'justify' it." He calls it "the sentiment of rationality," and we feel, he says, that it renders "the thing we think of *pro tanto* rational." He suggests that the theory and practice of reasoning, the collection of doctrines and disciplines we call logic, are but ways of a going whose goal is the sentiment, the awareness wherein "freedom" and "rationality" flow together into an ongoing ineffable "same" of duration. In relation to their goal the doctrines and disciplines are means, derivative, secondary, and contingent; they serve to set limits, to produce closures, to ordain stoppages that their devotees would preserve and repair but never alter, were it not that the élan—which they begin by channeling and end by damming—pervades them, at once the *terminus a quo* and the *terminus ad quem* of their formation; at once innovating, repeating, altering, transforming; alogical, logical, illogical; the twist, the spin, the whirl, the push and pull, of the struggle to keep on struggling which has survival for a synonym.

The sense of this élan, of this going which, so long as it lasts, has itself for its goal, this most nakedly immediate experience, may be what led Pascal to invoke "reasons of the heart" which the reason does not know. It seems more reliably what led William James to choose the ineffable rationality of freedom and give up the satisfying effable logic of the rationalists, whatever their denomination. In the crises of American history, it can plausibly be held to be not only that which led Theodore Parker, the abolitionist, to invoke the American Idea against the massed resistance of those for whom the American Dream had come true in his time. It can be held as well to have been the ongoing experience which Thomas Jefferson recalls in his *Dialogue Between My Head and My Heart*, that points up the stress of the choice between safety and freedom, the Dream and the Idea. "As far as my recollection serves me," Heart tells Head, "I do not know that I ever did a good thing on your suggestion, or a dirty one without it." For safety is not inseparable from life as freedom is, and as courage is inseparable from freedom. "If our country, when pressed with wrongs at the point of bayonet had been governed by its heads instead of its hearts, where should we be now? Hanging on a gallows as high as Haman's. You began to calculate and to compare wealth and numbers; we threw up a few pulsations of our blood, we supplied enthusiasm against wealth and numbers; we put our existence to the hazard when the hazard seemed against us and we saved our country, justifying at the same time the ways of Providence whose precept is to do always what is right and leave the issue to Him."

Awareness of the irreconcilable roads of freedom, one postulating the bondage of the different, the other the equal liberty of the different, could well have led Abraham Lincoln in his Second Inaugural to say of the War Between the States over issues which have survived the victory of the abolitionist North and are still being fought over: "All dreaded it, all sought to avert it. . . . Both parties deprecated war but one of them would *make* war rather than let the nation survive and the other would *accept* war rather than let it perish, and the war came"—even as other wars have come and keep coming, in terms of the walls which safety would build around freedom, the Dream around the Idea. It was during a deeply critical turn of that war for the North that Lincoln told his people: "The dogmas of the quiet past are inadequate to the stormy present. The occasion is piled high with difficulty, and we must rise to the occasion. As our case is new, so we must think and act anew. We must disenthrall ourselves. So we shall save our country."

The immuration of the Idea of Freedom by the Dream of Security, the Dreamer's aversion to taking account of the new and to thinking anew, is what the pragmatic intelligence, wherever it functions, must needs confront and overcome, and by overcoming, continue to disenthrall itself.

5 | "Group Libel" and Equal Liberty

Often, when I was a little boy, I would find myself in some sort of quarrel with playmates in which, sooner or later, we came to calling each other names. Before long, one or another of the name-callers would have exhausted his store of insults and would resort to a kind of chant, that I remember only as: "Sticks and stones may break my bones but names can never hurt me." There may have been other lines—I don't recall any. Nor have these sounded in my ears or risen in my fancy since I was ten or eleven years old. They came up unexpectedly after I began to think what I could say for the Law Forum about "group libel," and I have been wondering why so conspicuously obvious a contradiction of the facts of life should ever figure in children's ways of speech and what good it did or could do. Maybe Frazer[1] has found an explanation or some present or future cultural anthropologist will

[1] Sir James (George) Frazer (1854-1941), late Fellow of Trinity College, Cambridge.

76

seek out or invent one. Or perhaps the incantation came spontaneously from some child's mouth as a charm against the hurt a bad
name might inflict working evil like the "evil eye" against which
mankind's cultures have devised so many other charms besides
incantations.

For it is not true that names don't hurt, can't hurt. It is not
only a dog that can be hurt by a bad name. Every human being
can, and is. Call a person a Nazi, a Jew, a Communist, a bum, a
bastard, a lush, a son-of-a-bitch, a bag woman, a nigger, a quack, a
shyster, and so on and so on to no end; then, regardless of what in
fact he is, you assign him a character and a role which define
other people's expectations of his future behavior and predetermine their relations to him. Justifiably or not, you have made his
position among other people a hazard to him and handicapped his
struggle for a life and a living. You have dishonored him, and he
will do whatever is in his power to protect and revenge himself—
from responding to insult with greater insult to attacking with
fists or knives or guns.

In human relations, names are not only means of personal
identification; they are also instruments of offense and defense. Indeed, there is hardly a word or symbol in any language, hardly an
image in any culture, which is not usable as either a weapon or a
tool. Most can be as readily employed to hurt as to help, to destroy as to build up, to defame as to approve and exalt. Sometimes
merely uttering a proper name is an offense, like taking the name
of God "in vain." Saying "God" thus is now an offense little
regarded, a *maledicentia* or evil-saying, a blasphemy, at some
times, in some places, rightly to be punished with death.[2] But call
a man a Hitler or a Benedict Arnold or any other insulting name,
and instead of retorting in kind, he may challenge you to single
combat, knock you down, pull a knife on you or draw a gun.
Such reactions are spontaneous forms of the duello; we see them
on the television as a practice approved by the folkways and
mores which television "Westerns" immortalize. They have their
rules and rites. We see them observed by the gangs and other

[2] Years ago, I was myself charged with blasphemy under a Massachusetts
"blue law," which made the penalty death. I had said that if Sacco and Van-
zetti were anarchists, Jesus was an anarchist.

groups among whom they occur in the street fights of our cities, the grudge-fights in "clubs" and other hangouts, and so on. As fist-fights, they are arranged for among the military as the safest and surest way of finally settling a war of words. Their politest form is the ritual fight with long knives (swords) or pistols called the duel—once a delight of German Junkers and *couleur-studenten*, still resorted to by politicians in De Gaulle's France and in other countries with a tradition of chivalry. In this tradition, single combat or the duel is the gentleman's way of healing wounds to his honor. Their cure is infallibly a shedding of blood, if not a killing: victory vindicates the victor. One recalls the duel between Alexander Hamilton and Aaron Burr.

For whatever reason, public approval of one individual confronting another with sword or gun for the purpose of vindicating his wounded honor with bloody blows has become very rare. Even fist-fights, for honor and not profit, are deprecated, and the onlookers tend to apologize for their spontaneous pleasure in the irresistible spectacle, unless perhaps it is the still sanctioned defense of a woman's reputation. Duels have been widely forbidden by law and fighting them is considered a conspiratorial breach of the peace subject to police interference. Of course, rendering duels illegal was not the same as subjecting them to public disapproval. In some countries, duelling is still as acceptable as drinking bootleg liquor had been in the United States under the Eighteenth Amendment. And even where the law forbids duelling, the number, the variety, the intensity of hurts that libels aim to inflict are in no way diminished. The laws forbidding the customary remedy had, in the nature of things, to produce a substitute for it that the police-power—that is, the government's capacity for violence —could and would enforce. The substitute produced is the law of libel.

Invoking this law, the victim of any form of defamation may haul the aggressor into court and ask for damages or punishment or both, even in our United States, where our Bill of Rights assures speakers and writers that they may express themselves freely, without fear. For the first amendment provides no sanction for the hurts of name-calling and the Constitution provides only members of the Senate and the House, while performing their sworn duties, with immunity against lawful reprisal for slanders or libels they might thus perpetrate.[3] All others may be called to account on civil or criminal grounds, or both.

In more than one context, this was something new in human relations. Remedies by law for hurt from name-calling had not been available to victims who were identifiable as members of a social group—a class, a community, a race, a sex, a religious society, an occupation, a political party—possessing little property and less power. Unless one believes that a group as such is somehow like a person, that it sustains a sort of collective identity with an organic body and a living mind characteristically its own, a group as such cannot be hurt or helped. It would simply be a pattern of association for its members. It would simply be a voluntary organization that could be defamed or acclaimed only through its individual members.[4] Because only they, each alone or together with his fellows, have the capacity to feel and to think, to understand, to love and to hate, and to act on understanding and feelings, defensively or aggressively or both. They could resort to the courts severally, but not jointly, unless, perhaps, they had formed themselves into a juridical personality subject to corporate responsibility according to law. And such a personality is a legal fiction. That any member of a group not so incorporated and personalized should act, what he does and how much he does, depends a little on the intensity of his feelings of hurt, and a great

[3] U.S. Const. art. I, §6:

> The Senators and Representatives shall receive a Compensation for their Services, to be ascertained by Law, and paid out of the Treasury of the United States. They shall in all Cases, except Treason, Felony and Breach of the Peace, be privileged from Arrest during their Attendance at the Session of their respective Houses, and in going to and returning from the same; and for any Speech or Debate in either House, they shall not be questioned in any other Place.

[4] Beauharnais v. Illinois, 343 U.S. 250, 263 (1952). Mr. Justice Frankfurter in the majority decision states:

> It is not within our competence to confirm or deny claims of social scientists as to the dependence of the individual on the position of his racial or religious group in the community. It would, however, be arrant dogmatism . . . for us to deny that the Illinois legislature may warrantably believe that a man's job and his educational opportunities and the dignity accorded him may depend as much on the reputation of the racial and religious group to which he willy-nilly belongs, as on his own merits.

deal on what power he possesses and in what way and to what extent his fellow-members join their powers to his.

There is hardly a population which, whatever its numbers, does not include weak groups with little or no power who are belittled, treated as inferiors, as shiftless, wicked, unreliable, *und so weiter*. Although they may outnumber their more powerful "betters," their lacks reduce them to "minorities"—religious, ethnic, cultural, occupational. However they may feel about their imposed status, they may not safely express their feelings in public. What they say about the powerholders must at least seem to be respectful if not admiring, submissive and servile. To express themselves candidly about their joint and several *soi-disant* betters is tantamount to *lèse-majesté* in an autocracy: like naming a snake *Stalin* in Soviet Russia or a mongrel *Adolf* in Hitler's Germany, or a badger *Wallace* in Alabama, or a bedbug *Eastland* in Mississippi. If members of "minorities" spoke in this way of the "majority" they would be guilty of group libel, but group libel of the powerful by the powerless, and thus, false and blasphemous. Group libel is the privilege of rich and powerful "majorities."

The condition is global. All the world's cultures, the most "primitive" like the most "advanced," produce such patterns of group-libel. True, equals also libel each other; but the defamation of equals by equals is likely to be called group-prejudice, rather than libel or slander. So it is "prejudice," not libel for *soi-disant* communists to sneer at free societies as capitalist exploiters or imperialists or fascists, and for fascists to sneer at them as communists; it is "prejudice" for *soi-disant* democracies to sneer at authoritarian societies as fascist or communistic tyrannies. As the astounding rhetoric vented in the Assembly of the United Nations testifies, where there is no *force majeure* to call defaming powers to account, defamation is prejudice, not libel, and what is libel in the mouth of one power may be eulogy in the mouth of another. On occasion the libel or slander of a weak group by a stronger one may magnanimously be promoted to "prejudice"— as when we speak of "race prejudice," "religious prejudice" and the like. But changing the name does not affect the hurt and may aggravate it, like saying "colored" or "Negro" instead of "nigger," or "Hebrew" instead of "Jew." The intent remains libel; the purpose is to defame, and if the words as found in the dictionary are innocent, they are made guilty by the writer's style, by his so using them as to hurt those to whom they refer. Style is to libel often what tone of voice, facial expression, rhythm and accent of speech are to slander. The will to hurt, given voice, makes all the difference. As Mr. Justice Holmes observed in his dissent in the *Gitlow* case, "Every idea is an incitement. . . . The only difference between the expression of an opinion and an incitement . . . is the speaker's enthusiasm for the result," [5] and group libel more than other kinds.

Until the Democratic Revolution the multitudes of the people, alike as individuals and as members of diverse "minorities," ethnic, religious, occupational, and so on, had no defense against defamation, short of violence. Being poor and powerless, they had no rights their "betters" need respect. The latters' interests and attitudes imposed on the commoners their characters, their roles and their status, however these might be resented. The literature, arts, and theatre of the dominant culture projected the impositions in the form of caricatures and stereotypes of press and stage, and fastened them like iron masks upon the people they purported to portray. So, in the ways of the rich and powerful with the common people, libel was tantamount to truth; the mask *was* the man, and as often as not, the man became unable to distinguish himself from the mask. In its intent, the Democratic Revolution was more profoundly revolutionary than students of it realize, for it undertook to shake off and shatter the mask which property and power fastened on the poor and powerless. It proclaimed as self-evident the belief that however different individual men and their associations may be from one another, all are, *as different*, equal to one another in rights to "life, liberty and the pursuit of happiness" and that these rights are unalienable. It set itself to shape up a society which should give effect to its proclamation by converting the terms of it from articles of faith into facts of life— that is, it drew up a design for a political and cultural economy whose laws should assure to the different, *as different*, equal liberty and equal safety.

Obviously, even in our United States, the land of its origin,

[5] Gitlow v. New York, 268 U.S. 652, 673 (1923).

and where it may rightly be said to have made greater progress, the Democratic Revolution is still unfinished and, in the nature of things, will stay so, however greatly it prospers. Equality in right is not the same as equality in power; and in a free society, justice demands equality in power before the law. Injustice thrives on inequality, so that the pursuit of justice is a struggle for equalization before the law; mostly, the task of the courts, the police power, and the administration of laws of a democracy is to secure equality in freedom and rights by preventing injustice.

This, by and large, is what the Bill of Rights is for, especially the first amendment and its bearing on the laws of libel. For on observing this amendment depends the safeguarding of all other rights. It makes the poor and powerless equal with the propertied and powerful to write and speak freely and safely. It assures this equality by committing the hitherto biased power of government to supporting and protecting the rights of the weak, and thus, redressing the historical imbalance in favor of the strong. The law of libel similarly assures the poor the revolutionary right to invoke the law in public defense against the hurts of libel; it sets them free to fight back and to demand amends. But it frees them sheerly as individuals, not as members of a group who have been made the victims of libel because they are members of this group and identified by traits attributed to it. Imagine a Jew suing for libel because he is vilified by being described as a Jew, or a Negro by being described as a Negro. What is lawfully open to him is to join together with others libelously so described and to watch for, challenge, and refute the libels as they appear; to expose their origins, their supporters and their motivations. This is what the B'nai Brith made of its Anti-Defamation League, what the American Jewish Congress and other Jewish organizations were among the first to attempt. Since, all sorts of "minority" groups have set up similar voluntary "anti-defamation" agencies.

In more senses than one, their programs might be said to exemplify in practice Mr. Justice Brandeis' observation in his dissent in *Whitney v. California*, "If there be time to expose through discussion the falsehood and fallacies, to avert the evil by the processes of education, the remedy to be applied is more speech, not enforced silence." [6] But who is to decide whether or not there is time? By what measure? What led the Illinois courts to convict Beauharnais under the State statute forbidding any kind of publication which exposes "the citizen of any race, color, creed or religion to contempt, derision, or obloquy or is productive of breach of the peace or riots?" [7] Beauharnais, a racist white, had defamed not *a* Negro, *the* Negro. Convicted, he appealed and carried his appeal all the way to the Supreme Court which affirmed the conviction, five to four, Mr. Justice Frankfurter writing the decision of the majority cited above.[8] But no Federal law against group libel has been enacted, nor, so far as I know, has any state followed Illinois' example. As I read their statements, the basic issue between the majority of five and the minority of four is the intent they attribute to the first amendment. Is it absolute or modified by time, place and circumstances: by occasions, say, when publication would create a clear and present, not a remote and possible danger? Must the present be instant, or may it follow after a stretch of time? How long a stretch?

The answers to such questions would be obvious if it could be agreed that the words used—as a unanimous Supreme Court observed in *Chaplinsky v. New Hampshire*[9]—were words which

[6] 274 U.S. 357, 377 (1927).

[7] Ill. Laws [1917] 362, §1 (June 29, 1917), Ill. Rev. Stat., ch. 38, §471 (1949) (repealed 1961). The present form of the statute is worded differently, Ill. Annot. Stats., ch. 38, §27-1 (1961):

> (a) A person commits criminal defamation when, with intent to defame another, living or dead, he communicates by any means to any person matter which tends to provoke a breach of the peace.

The reason for the change in wording is explained in the Committee Comments to Article 27:

> [I]t rejects the idea of punishing communications which tend merely to injure reputation, and specifically makes the gist of the crime the tendency to provoke breaches of the peace. The Committee felt that insofar as the law of criminal libel was designed to compensate for or to mitigate the injury to the victim's reputation, it has completely failed. In addition the criminal law should generally not be used to remedy private wrongs. A tort action for libel or slander is more appropriate and more effective. Consequently, the theoretical justification for criminal defamation is grounded entirely on the prevention of breaches of the peace.

[8] Supra note 4.

[9] 315 U.S. 568 (1942).

"by their very utterance inflict injury or tend to incite an immediate breach of the peace." [10] Such words are still speech, not action. But they stop discussion and prevent education. Do they or
do they not figure in themselves as breaches of the peace, incitements to riot? Is their utterance protected by the first amendment? To forbid it is to be guilty of "prior restraint," to practice
censorship, and thus to create precedents with the cumulative
effect of endangering equal liberty. Not to forbid it is to open the
way to violence and the destruction of public order and safety.
The English, who since World War II have had to admit into
their tight, white little island, thousands of dark-skinned fellow
Britishers from various regions that still are or recently were parts
of the British Commonwealth, prefer order and public safety to
equal liberty, and by implication, "prior restraint" and censorship. So, by and large, do most of the freer countries, while in
totalitarian countries, freedom is not an alternative. So far, it is
only in the United States that the people are betting on equal
liberty, discussion and education as against "prior restraint," censorship and other uses of the public power in behalf of "law and
order." They are betting that in the long run the former are more
effective than the latter in dissipating group-libel, defeating the
purposes of the libelous and preserving "law and order." They
have come to believe that:

> [T]he ultimate good desired is better reached by free trade in
> ideas—that the best test of truth is the power of thought to get it
> self accepted in the competition of the market, and that truth is
> the only ground upon which their wishes safely can be carried out.
> That at any rate is the theory of the Constitution. It is an experi
> ment, as all life is an experiment. Every year if not every day we
> have to wager our salvation upon some prophecy based upon im
> perfect knowledge. While that experiment is part of our system
> I think that we should be eternally vigilant against attempts to
> check expression of opinions that we loathe and believe to be
> fraught with death, unless they so imminently threaten immediate
> interference with the lawful and pressing purposes of the law that
> an immediate check is required to save the country.[11]

10 Id. at 572.
11 Abrams v. United States, 250 U.S. 616, 630 (1919) (Holmes, J., dissenting).

But the question persists: If the threat is not in itself an act of violence, who shall decide and how shall he decide that the threat is immediate and should be immediately checked? Are not such decisions, like all others, bets and not a sure thing?

6 | Majorities, Minorities and National Solidarity

Every war, hot or cold, brings its anxieties, and thus charges and counter-charges, suspicions, division, and the release of a natural propensity among power-holders, to project their own deficiencies as others' sins, and their own fears as others' betrayals. The disposition to exceed becomes unrestrained, and rational prudence gets blown up into the hysterias and hypocrisies we today call mccarthyism. Some problems, e.g., of the Negroes and of other religious, cultural or ethnic "minorities," are due to chronic injustice, prejudice and exploitation, and can be readily enough solved by admitting the people thus shut out to full and equal participation in civil defense and the war effort. Equal opportunity to contribute their utmost to security or victory is what the people desire; they in no way desire giving aid and comfort to the enemy.

Problems of national solidarity of this order belong to quite another family than those posed by groups who would, at least, prefer to see the enemy undefeated and a peace without victory or a cold war, while at most they would help and welcome an enemy victory. Such groups obstruct the work for security by word and deed, and in varying degrees do aid the enemy. In World War One, Woodrow Wilson denounced them as hyphenated Americans. In World War Two they have been known successively as American Firsters, Christian Fronters, Copperheads, Fifth Columnists.

Although both World Wars started as assaults upon peaceable mankind by an identical foe proclaiming an essentially identical faith, the two wars so differed in range, intensity, scope and technique as to be different in kind. The First was a ruthless aggression by an imperialist sovereign to whom international treaties were scraps of paper, and national honor a craven superstition. The Second War was the total assault on the peaceful peoples by piratical sadistocrats for whose malice no torture was too cruel, no crime too foul. Woodrow Wilson said that we were at war "to make the world safe for democracy." Franklin Roosevelt said that we were fighting "for survival." The difference between "safety" and "survival" suggests something of the difference between the nation's foes and the nation's tasks in the two wars. It implies that with the foe of the First War it would have been possible to come to some understanding; that there was room in the world for him and for us; that the rule of *live and let live* might apply after that war as it applied before. It suggests that with the foe of the Second War, the opposite was the case. By faith and by works, if the Japonazi was not an aggressor, he was nothing at all. The rule that he imposed on us was *kill or be killed;* he would have no room in his "new world order" for both him and us. So we fought him for survival.

Now we have been engaged, morally on a global scale, materially in Korea, in Burma, in Indochina, in Berlin, upon a third world war. As a generic struggle, it is still a "cold" war, being fought in the chancelleries of the nations and the councils of U.N. As a specific struggle it is hot and bloody wherever the soldiers of freedom and the bondsmen of totalitarian communism or racism or sacerdotalism confront each other with arms. Even more than the Second World War, the Third is a war for survival.

Is Every Minority Traitorous?

Though some would-be presidents imply the opposite, it should be needless to affirm that this survival is not, cannot be, inertly continued existence. As Santayana wrote somewhere, "Nothing can be meaner than the anxiety to live on, to live on any how, in any shape; a spirit with any honor is not willing to live except in its own way." In peace, no less than in war, it is for the survival of the American Idea that the American people are today pledging their lives, their fortunes and their sacred honors: for the idea of the free way of a free society whose habits and ideals make, of each and every one of the miscellany of the world who together form the solidary American people, in and out an American.

Because we fought, and fight, not for the safety but for the survival of the American Idea, national solidarity continues an imperative with an import which World War One did not know. How we perceive it, how we maintain and enhance it, become issues of maximum importance to our happy as well as victorious survival. That it involves the common will to victory goes without saying. Groups and individuals lacking this will or willing the opposite present no problem. They cut themselves off from the national solidarity and set themselves against it. And the nation and its police-agencies must prevent them from ever harming the national solidarity. Alike, past experience and present experiment agree on how to deal with minorities who oppose and seek to foment division in the nation's will and way freely to maintain its freedoms.

The difficulties come, not in the relations of "minorities" who are *opposed*, but in the relations of "minorities" who are *different*, and whom custom and precedent have penalized for being thus different, even in a free society like ours, whose faith is embodied in the Declaration of Independence, the intent of whose works is the Constitution and its Amendments. Both faith and works affirm the parity of the different. If the Declaration says that all men are created equal, it does not mean equal in spite of differences of faith or race or sex or occupation, but equal *as different* in faith or race or sex or occupation; it affirms the right to be different, the equal right of different persons in the common struggle for the diversities of life, liberty and the pursuit of happiness, to secure which, governments have been instituted among men.

If the Bill of Rights and the subsequent Amendments forbid Congress to make certain laws, they forbid Congress to penalize differences, whether of religion, of thought, of expression, of sex, of ownership, of occupation and the like. Franklin Roosevelt summed up both the faith and the working plan of the American way as "the Four Freedoms"; freedom of speech and expression, of conscience, freedom from want, from fear—everywhere in the world. In brief, freedom, whatever be its field, is a synonym for the right to be and to become different. Harry Truman struggled in a diverse way to bring this faith to fact and this plan to act. Dwight Eisenhower has repeated his affirmations of the faith; but there is as yet no public record of things done to make it fact. All three know well that a free society is not a fixed order of sames but a mobile association of differents. The solidarity of the diverse and ever-diversifying members of such a society is expressed by the division of labor and the unity of faith and purpose resulting from the spontaneous orchestration of all their many differences. At the moment the most urgent, the most tragic, problem of our solidarity certain privileged minorities have put in differences of race. Because of them, the nation as a whole has been brutally penalizing our Negro fellow-citizens for their difference in color, our Mexican and Indian fellow-citizens for their difference of culture as well.

In suffering this, we are conforming to the standards of the foe whom we must convince or overthrow, if we are not to be overthrown by him. In suffering this we are ourselves assaulting the American Way whose survival we are said to be defending. We are wiping out the difference between Washington and Moscow and justifying the charges of Peking and New Delhi. By omission and commission we are setting mccarthyism against the democratic faith we purport to defend. As Franklin Roosevelt told the Association for the Advancement of Colored People on February 3, 1943: "The principle on which this country was founded and by which it has always been governed is that Americanism is a matter of mind and heart. It is not, and never was, a matter of race or ancestry."

Where Is Our Solidarity?

America's solidarity, it follows, is likewise a matter of mind and heart. It consists in the teamplay of all the people in their personal being and in their associative combinations. Each, as person or as group, counts as One, and by itself alone, as a minority of One. Each is a One different from all the other Ones, and endeavoring to live and work and play with the others as an equal neighbor, hoping through this free communion with the different to attain a better life than any One could by himself alone. Because the nation is an associative One, is the living Union of these many different lesser Ones, each holding freely together with the others; because the nation is not merely one "race" or one "faith" or one "class" maintaining itself as an "elite" by force and fraud which keeps other groups down, the national solidarity gets a material strength greater than the sum of its parts, and a spiritual richness more variedly abundant than the total of its "human resources." Its psyche is expressed in the national maxim —*E Pluribus Unum*—out of the Many, One; the Life of the One being the common way created by the union of the separate and distinct works and ways of the Many.

The nation's religious denominations, trade unions and managements, educational establishments, have recently begun to acknowledge and affirm this pluralism intrinsic to the nation's life and culture. By their "interfaith" and "intercultural" enterprises they have been giving the spontaneous and unconscious self-orchestration of some of the nation's diverse communions of interest, conscious self-realization and direction. Recall the words of Mr. Harold B. Hoskins of the State Department, repeating more than a decade ago an insight as old as Jefferson, and the intent of the American Ideal: "As many speakers and writers have begun to suggest, our American ideal should be expressed not in terms of a 'melting pot' with its somewhat mournful implication of uniformity, but rather of an orchestra where each racial group contributes its special different tone to the rich ensemble of the whole." To the Department of State as it then spoke, the ideal *E Pluribus Unum*, the principle of the orchestration of mankind, had to become an instrument of global policy, the only one that could effectively counter the monolithic imperialism of the totalitarians—be they purple, red, brown or black. Americans are more and more aware that only insofar as American society disciplines itself to this principle and realizes itself in this ideal, it continues as a free society and its diversified enterprises continue as free enterprise. And the Universal Declaration of Human Rights adopted by the Assembly of the United Nations expressed this awareness for all the world's peoples.

When Democracy Succeeds

A free society makes Liberty the foundation of Union, and Union the guarantee of Liberty. In the degree that it does so successfully, it is a democracy. Now, in democracies majorities and minorities do not possess the fixed and static character with which tradition and the mores everywhere are disposed to endow them and which authoritarian institutions everywhere in the world, from Vatican City to Moscow and Peking, from Cairo to New Delhi, from Buenos Aires to Madrid, endeavor to impose and to perpetuate as law and as fact. In democracies minorities combine into majorities; and majorities divide into minorities. They are ever changing in numbers, power, importance. One is always passing over into the other; and each respects the other's right, one by the use of reason to accomplish, the other by the use of reason to resist this passage, if it can. If a trades-union, a learned society, a corporation, an ethnic, cultural or religious group or its members are counted minority units in one connection, they may become majority units in another. The distinction between majority and minority is associative and functional, not organic, not constitutive.

In the end, all majorities are large associations of individuals primarily coming together in lesser associations of minorities.

Their relations and memberships are in a continuous flux of union and separation. In politics, we think of the relation between our majority and minority parties as a competition and argument in the public service wherein the majority may become the minority and the minority may make itself the majority. When a minority seeks the nullification and defeat of the way of life which freely permits and protects it, we declare it subversive and its rights forfeit. Recently under the impact of authoritarian cash and creeds, sectional passion, personal vendetta, and commercial lust, many such subversive minorities have taken form. More than once, legislative halls exemplify the definition of patriotism in Samuel Johnson's Dictionary.

Since majority and minority relationships enter our experience most vividly via the necessary rivalries and disputations of political parties, we Americans are inclined to think of all majority-minority relationships as competition and argument. To our propensity to think of associations and groups as fixed and static we add a tendency to fear difference and to confuse it with conflict. The sociologist's word for this tendency is "Xenophobia." It disposes us to accept likeness even when it comes to us with intent to enslave or kill. It disposes us to shut out and fight off difference, no matter how much this may enrich and strengthen us. The behavior, the feelings, the blind, unconscious subversion of the American Idea whereto this disposition leads us make up the crises of national solidarity wherein resides the perennial domestic challenge of the American faith and way. These feelings, this behavior, are dangerous sicknesses of democracy. In history they have gone by many names, of which the most widely used has been "Knownothingism." They name a mentality that is the problem of the majority, not the minority. Chronic in times of peace, wartimes make it acute, and its healing becomes a major task of those charged with organizing security or victory.

Recall the attitude of the Irish Free State toward the United Kingdom during the Second World War. Bitter memories of oppression caused an unsympathetic "neutrality" which endangered that State's own survival. Recall the difference between the fighting spirit of the Philippines and of the peoples of Burma, Malaya, Indochina, South Africa. Relatively the Filipinos had been treated as free men, different from ourselves, but equal in the partnership of the different wherein the unity of our free society consists. The darker peoples of Burma and the Indochina other lands had not been thus treated. The Filipinos remain our staunch allies and comrades committed to fighting in peace and war for the Four Freedoms.

But how much could the Four Freedoms really have meant, or mean, to the Burmese, Malayans, Vietnamese, Hindus, South Africans? And what can they mean especially to our own dark-skinned fellow-citizens, north and south, in the fields, factories, army, navy, if there they are penalized because different?

Americans who honestly believe in the American Idea have the duty to establish as practice as well as profession the national solidarity which consists in the teamwork of the different and which depends on the equality of the different in right as well as in duty toward the common task. On the battlefield, in the production plants, in the Courts, in Congress, in the State Legislatures, and in the places of amusement and recreation, the duty is the same. The Americanization of Americans at home is indispensable to the acceptance abroad of the ideal of equal liberty for the different and the cooperation of the different on equal terms. It is the *sine qua non* for communion in peace, for victory in war, and security at all times.

7 | Democracy in a World of Tensions

Ambiguity and Misuse

I sincerely doubt whether any fruitful results can come out of an analysis of the "ambiguities" of the word "democracy." I do not believe that the word is ambiguous to any of its users; nor do honest users regard themselves as guilty of misuse. The divergencies between the senses the word is used in by politically opposed users cannot be traced to any kind of "misuse" unless insincerity or malice is evidenced. These constitute all that can properly be meant by "misuse." Now, I do believe that certain modifications in the meaning of "democracy" have become current which tend to effect a mutation from the original intention of the word. Those are due almost entirely to Russian practice, and honest people in other parts of the world have taken over the usage. While I prefer to continue to mean by "democracy" the program initially defined by Jefferson and implemented more or less successfully since his time, I would prefer to let the processes of usage take care of themselves. If the alternative meaning became current, I would try to find another word for the spiritual and behavioral realities for which "democracy" seems generally to be a name. I regard the semantic question as being only incidentally an independent variable. When ideals are merely professions and not programs, it is possible to talk about them as the Sidney Webbs talked about the Russian Constitution. When ideals are programs, they exist in various stages of actualization and "the fight for the ideal" is obviously a fight for whatever in fact actualizes it and not for a label merely.

Social versus Political Democracy

I reject the idea of any out and out opposition between "social democracy and political democracy." I think the difference is one of scope and range, but not of character. In Lincoln's formulation, "government of the people, by the people, for the people," the intention of the word "government" must be taken to cover every mode of organization intended to direct behavior. Whatever be the character of the association—political, economic, religious, cultural, recreational, educational, sexual, and what have you—in which people who are different from each other undertake to live together with each other, the basis of the association is voluntary participation by all concerned in the goals, the methods, and the alterations of the control of the common enterprise. This is not true of Russia, even when you accept Sidney Webb's interpretation of the Russian view of "democracy." The facts of record certainly do not bear out this interpretation of Webb's, since the Russian association is not voluntary and the interests of the majority are not determined by the majority but by a ruling "élite."

From what I have already said it should be obvious that I decline to make a rule as to how the word "democracy" should be used by others. The fact is that it is sometimes applied to limited areas of behavior and sometimes to very extensive ones, and that there is a disposition always to broaden the field of application. It is a matter of record that where "political democracy" obtains people are disposed to employ their political power in order to extend the democratic relation to other fields. As to priorities, there is no evidence yet of "social democracy" leading to "political democracy" while there is evidence of "political democracy" finding extension to "social democracy." As to which is means or which is an end, the answer would depend on the sequence of events. There is no intrinsic quality which requires either to be one thing or the other. What particular pattern of social organization may follow a political pattern seems to me rather a matter of will and purpose than a matter of logical or dialectical necessity. This is particularly valid, I think, in respect to "the socialization of the means of production." Such a process might be the enemy of political liberty as well as a reinforcement of it. When the liberals and conservatives reacted against the idea that "democracy" had economic and social implications it was because, like Socialists, they were concerned about either the holding or the extension of their own powers and privileges. It is now customary to speak of "democratic socialism" so as to distinguish it from communism. Thus the Soviets validate the distinction quoted from de Tocqueville; the British may invalidate it; our own TVA does invalidate it. That men first proposed socialism as an instrument of freedom and now use it as a rationalization of tyranny indicates that "socialism" is as viable a term as "democracy." If you take Bryce's conception of "democracy" as "merely a form of government" and take it to apply to all governments, religious and economic and educational as well as political, you can accept it as far as it goes. But it is obviously not compatible with the propositions of the American Declaration of Independence.

It should be obvious that I do not believe that you can separate "democracy" from liberty. I regard "democracy" as an organization of liberty, anywhere and everywhere. When controversialists such as de Tocqueville and Lenin separate them, they do so not as disinterested observers, but as debaters making special pleas. The terms they select and how they use them are functions of the interests they are endeavoring to serve. Whether these interests are called "real" or illusory depends on who makes the call. Obviously, to no party at interest who is honest and sincere can his interest be illusory. When a diversity of interests are in play, if discussion is free and full, it either comes to a conclusion in a consensus or in a division into majority and minority. The criterion is created by the terminus reached, and it obtains, in a free society, until free and full discussion changes opinion again.

Such discussion, of course, implies a maximum of knowledge. When you speak of a body of voters 80 per cent of whom "were kept in conditions of minimal intellectual independence, etc." you are not talking about a "democratic" society. If, on the other hand, the 80 per cent *kept themselves* in that condition, making no effort to change it, they could very well be "democratic." The difference would turn on the effort to obtain access to alternatives of thought, opinion, etc. Bona fide presentation of alternatives under rules of free communication would be "democratically justifiable." This becomes a guide to drawing the line between "democratic" and "non-democratic" delegation of power. The "democratism" reaches an optimal level in consensus, down to majority. In this country it can be prevented by a senatorial filibuster, and both are subject to continuous checking by a public opinion which depends on an untrammeled right to speak and to *listen* for the drawing of conclusions.

Tolerance and Treason

What I have just said points to what I believe to be involved in the rights of opposition. On this point I know of nothing in the record which makes it necessary or desirable to modify the position taken by John Stuart Mill in his essay "On Liberty." It is clear that without a thorough understanding of alternatives the growth and defense of "democracy" is handicapped. The limit is reached where the intention of the alternative is manifestly the destruction of "democracy." Just as, according to Mill, a free man cannot logically choose slavery since he thus chooses the destruction of his freedom, so a free society is not required by its own logic to facilitate its own destruction. The limits are obviously those of the "clear and present danger" invoked by the late Mr. Justice Holmes. That this process is difficult, no one denies, but, on the whole, the American way has not done badly in the handling of the problem of the limits of freedom; and it is well to remember that perfect, fool-proof solutions are possible only to God, who has very carefully chosen his confidants regarding these. So far, "democrats" are not among them. In the United States the objection is rather to the violence of change than to the nature of change; but I should myself prefer to oppose any change which cut off the freedom to continue to make changes. In the United States the lines of change are defined in terms of the Declaration of Independence, the Constitution and its amendments, and now also the United Nations Organization with its Bill of Human Rights, etc. These, with their acquiescence in the plurality and diversity of individuals and societies and the right of each to life, liberty, and the pursuit of happiness, would make it necessary to rule out the imposition of a one-party political system. None such can be compatible with a "democratic" form of government, whatever be the area, religious, economic, etc., no less than political. From this it follows obviously that even if there were infallible opinions they could lose nothing of their power and validity if fallible alternatives had every opportunity to survive or perish on their merits in the open market of political opinion. In fact, a demand for "universal allegiance" is a sign of a lack of faith in the power of a doctrine to win and hold allegiance on its own merits. The infallible should be able to survive the challenge of inquiry and the test of experiment without any other help, and skepticism of it could only serve, when free and competent, to vindicate it. Thus the uses of skepticism are correlative to the uses of faith, and the one faith which I regard as indispensable to "democracy" is a faith in freedom. Generally, intolerance is a sign of insecurity, or a concealed or overt skepticism of one's own doxy.

The Value Foundations of the Conflict

I regard all value-judgments as ultimately as irreducible as the individuals who make them. In the course of the daily life they are functions of the judges far more than the judges are functions of them. People like to diminish or destroy some aspects of their experience and preserve or expand others. They start, from where they are, to alter it by transformations of this kind. They speak of these transformations as "ought" and "duty." Sometimes they are in the position of two men trying to marry the same girl. They might create a world in which the girl could be the wife of both of them; or they might stay in a world in which they have to fight each other for her possession; or one might care enough about the girl to give her up to the other; or the girl might reject both. The "oughts" in these alternatives would develop as rationalizations of the passions in play. There have been events in history, especially those known as religious wars, where alternatives have been analogous. They could even be extended to the bitter refusal of some sects to eat meat and to insist on vegetables, or to wear their hair in one way and not another for the glory of God. There is no use talking, in such situations, about "primarily local cravings" as against "basic differences." The Civil War between the Big-Enders and the Little-Enders in Lilliput could be called a matter of "local cravings" rather than "basic differences in values"; but it was a Civil War just the same, and wherever individuals or societies are ready to risk their lives for some mode of thought or behavior the issue is "basic" enough.

So when it comes to suppressing Fascists and not Communists or Communists and not Fascists, there is a matter of preference and passion more or less explicit. In terms of the "democratic" process, repression weakens "democracy" by keeping it unready. Its stability is not so much a function of the elimination of the infection as it is development of antibodies which neutralize and check the infection. It is this process which makes immunity in matters of health, and I believe the same thing to be true with respect to "democracy."

I do not believe that "ideological controversies" are ever "assuaged." Like the controversy over evolution, they are dropped because one alternative has been able to do the job in which it claimed proficiency better than its competitor. There are few direct conversions on the mere logical merits of an issue. Sometimes a common enemy may lead to co-operative defensive action from which positive co-operative action may stem. It was certainly hoped for when Russia and the Allies were "united" against Hitler. A natural catastrophe such as an earthquake might also lead to defensive and remedial co-operation which could spread out into continuous, positive, constructive collaboration. But it is also possible that one of the opponents might point to the event with delight as the judgment of God and, instead of helping, gloat. Sometimes the most that can be expected is that the rivals shall live together in each other's presence in a sort of painful toleration, or it may be that the kind of practice of *live and let live* and even *live and help live* may develop that is achieved by the Protestant sects through the Federal Council of Churches and that is intended by the Charter of the United Nations. Again, doctrine may here be entirely contradictory to discipline, as the teachings of many Christian sects exemplify and, of course, the whole Marxist gospel. The facts of record and the doctrinal pretension are polar opposites to each other. Hence, whether there be any "incompatibility" between Lenin's *terminus ad quem* and other people's does not make any difference in the working relationships. But there is an incompatibility for the very reason that you cannot separate the way of reaching the goal from the goal reached. The going creates the goal, whatever be the language in which it is described.

It is said that there are more than four billion people alive on the globe today, and that however numerously they die, their numbers are increasing. It is recognized that none succeeds in staying alive by himself alone. However much he segregates himself, he must associate with others of his genus in order not to die. A baby left to itself would certainly perish; a hermit without other persons concerned at least to feed him would starve to death—a monastery could be called a society of mutually supporting hermits. On every level, segregation is artificial and sophisticated, the loner is a sick soul; the natural man is a social man. The natural man is one, in a family with father, mother, brothers and sisters and other blood relations. His family make-up is one in a tribe, a community, and so on. He himself is a one in all the groups, the ultimate unit in the total aggregation we call humanity. He figures in each of them to the degree that he commits himself to its collective aims and to the means that it uses to attain its aims—the foremost ones being always securing the necessities of life and exercising the various arts meant to provide the necessities not only.

What is taken for necessity is established by the diversity of the group's aims and by the variety and effectiveness of the occupations pursued to attain the aims. Hence the truism that the necessities of an industrial civilization outnumber those of a primitive culture. The latter can keep alive without the immeasurable variety of knowings and skills which it would first atrophy and finally kill a modern society to do without. If we ask ourselves, or our neighbors, who we are, as one in the aggregate of other people among whom we live and work and play and fight, what would each answer? In what terms—the feeling of our separate selfhood? of our awareness of living on from instant to instant, hour to hour, day to day? our making up the story of our selfhood as our present experience is made into our past memory by our growing older? Or do we answer those questions about our identity in terms of our relations with other identities? Doesn't every definition a person makes of himself postulate such relations? Son, daughter, parent, doctor, lawyer, Indian chief, policeman, poet, prizefighter, teacher, student, hippie, yippie, politician, statesman, priest, scientist, trade unionist, capitalist, communist, fascist, nazi, democrat, lover, dove, hawk—to mention only a few of the countless variety of self-designations—are words of relation. They identify us by our transactions with other people. They signify social roles we play although we don't play even the most characteristic all the day every day of our lives. We learn our roles as we grow up and grow older, assume them, drop them in many cases as we put on and take off our garments. Not many stage-actors become the characters they play, but the playing does leave a residue in the personality of the man, and we perceive him as actor even off stage. Some of any man's roles do endure and shape his future, others are recessive, still others are intermittent or incidental. But all turn on his relations with other persons and with the non-human materials and tools by which those relations are entered into, maintained, ordered or altered.

The personal history of each of us, as a biographer might compose it, shapes up as the shifts and changes of these relations with the coming years. It signifies identity as a unique process in time, ever creating the form of selfhood the person aspires to be, and more or less recognized and treated as such by other persons. Aspirations, of course, look to the future; they are disclosed in what the aspirer presently says and how he says it, what he does and how he does it. Explicit or implicit, they signify the creed and code of his personal faith—they signify, that is, those of his judgements of existence and value on which he bets his life, for which he might make "the supreme" as well as any other, sacrifice, laying down his life for his God—or his girl or his money or his dope, or his country or his crap game or golf game or any of the commonly accepted or commonly rejected values that men do lay down their lives for. The ultimate proof of a true believer's commitment to his belief is what he risks in order to bring it to event, in order to make and keep it incarnate in reality. His risk discloses whether his aspiration is fantasy or purpose, profession or practice, as Tory Dr. Samuel Johnson, resenting the practices of certain Whig politicians, gave evidence in his famous Dictionary, when he defined patriotism as the last resort of a scoundrel.

But what has not been similarly excommunicated—science by religionists, religions by rival religions and by science, any way of life, any establishment—economic, political, cultural—by some rebel or dissident and conversely? The fear, the hatred, the excommunication and quarantining of otherness is far more apparent than their reciprocal inclusion in the course of their struggles—each for its own survival, literally its own out-living—of the circumambient others also struggling to live on and not die. True, killing abolishes individuality beyond replacement; but short of killing, it continues ever under the greatest duress to strive to preserve itself. Whatever destructive changes its environment may impose, and however much it may seem outwardly to accept them, it never takes them substantially to heart and mind. From its psychosomatic core ever-expanding outward, individuality rings itself with defenses against being overpowered and outlived by the circumambience of human and non-human forces which it must overcome in order merely to keep alive.

But keeping merely alive from birth to death is not the same as development out of infancy into old age. The existence of all animals is a struggle to grow up and grow older. Animal bodies breathe in order to keep on breathing, feed in order to keep on feeding, and so on and on. And humans are first, last and always, animals; let any of our vital organs cease to function and at least as bodies we cease to be. Our organic animal functions are tantamount to our original power of survival, and first and last we experience power as the exercise of our animal functions. The power we exercise as human supervenes upon our animal power, supplements it, displaces it, and works in quite other ways—ways which such words as *spirit, soul, culture, civilization,* signify. They are ways which endow a human society, however small or large, with its identity. Its struggle for survival as *this* society is its struggle to nourish, diversify and pass on these ways. Its success or failure comes with how the individuals whose togetherness sustains it relate to their common environment and to each other— comes, that is, with increase or decrease of the range and scope of the communication between them regarding the human and non-human scene of their joint and several strivings to live on, growing. Perhaps the entire process has its ongoing impulsion in the fact that man the animal is not born a human but only may become human: that his humanness is a possibility of his bodily organization which may or may not become actual, even as an actual egg may or may not become an actual chick. The alteration happens only if the outer world sets it going and favors its consummation. So, without the care and help of the already human, no infant could survive nor could it get started and sustained toward the consummation of its humanity. Parents, nurses, elder brothers, teachers, physicians, priests, friends and fellow students all purport to help us grow up as humans while we are growing older as animals, until we are able to do for ourselves what our helpers have been doing for us.

But the time never comes when we can dispense with all help. For human beings even death—especially death—requires the helping hand of others. Most of us shrink from dealing with our dead by ourselves alone. That this need of care—need of the infant, need of the helpless, need of the very old—is resented even while served, is of course a part of the human record. Ancient societies such as the Hellenic or the Roman, for example, once practiced abandoning infants judged unable to grow up into self-care and self-help. Others outlawed—some still do—the aged who have become similarly unable. Civilization is sometimes measured by the scope and effectiveness of public concern for all the very young and all the very old. A scarcity of such concern gets deprecated and condemned: laws get passed and acted on for the protection and care of both. The laws serve as units in the public means of achieving public ends which get redefined with the overall increase of reliable knowledge and the diversification of its uses. The increase signalizes an increase in human power while the animal power which the expression "man-power" names stays the same or diminishes. What, then, is this human power experienced as? All human animals strive for power other than that animal force (which they automatically resist and fight to overcome) of the aggressive world around, or which they themselves exert aggressively to satisfy their needs and wants. This other power is experienced as knowledge.

The identity of this power with knowledge was first shown by Francis Bacon; the maxim, *"knowledge is power"* is his. Not that men were not immensely knowledgeable when he thus identified power. But although they believed that what they believed they knew could work wonders for them, and employed it as weapon and tool of their struggles to keep on struggling, they found that in comparison with the kind of knowledge Bacon said is power, their kind was impotent to bring them greater abundance or greater security or greater liberty in a world made no more for them than for any other form of life. Impressed by a certain distrust and misprision of this neutral universe and impelled by a strong desire to be saved from its pervasive inhumanities, they constructed this non-Baconian knowledge of theirs from ineffable articles of faith and rules of conduct regarding how to die out of the natural world into a supernatural one where the true believer could resume his living-on certain that he would be free, safe and satisfied forever. The rules prescribed his accepting and enhancing the scarcities and sufferings of earth as the way of laying up the more abundant treasure of heaven forever.

But the survival which this knowledge enabled is not the survival actually achieved, not living on where one is as one is, but living on after one is dead, in another place and in bodiless form.

The kind of knowledge which Francis Bacon found to be power is, on the other hand, knowledge of the world we live in before we die, knowledge which we gain by the methods and the skills that in due course become "science." Whatever else "science" may mean, it means also that enormous diversification of learning and using the stuffs and forms of the world around us so as to render them ever more human means to human ends. They are non-human power—horse power, water power, steam power, electric power, atom power, electronic power, replacing man-power—each and every one a containing of a form of nature's energy in a human contrivance which harnesses and drives it in the service of human purposes. Knowledge is man's overall harnessing of nature's powers. Uncontained, unharnessed, these powers serve no purpose, they spend themselves to no end, unless the suicide of entropy be a true end and not the dead end it is. Nature's free flow to entropy is not self-conservation but self-destruction. Only as its quanta are contained, harnessed and put to work is their sequence of destruction transvalued into the force of creation.

Harnessing up and employing the powers of nature humanizes and civilizes them. It follows from taking them as sequences of cause and effect and from foreseeing and achieving effects by means of controlling and directing their causes. Effects are chosen in the belief that they serve to prolong human life, to diversify it, enrich it, and render it ever more abundant; and that they cut off and shut out powers which oppose this while opening up to and including powers which facilitate it. The overall end is the process of human survival as growth. If we appraise the process in terms of life-expectancy of members of the different societies of mankind, we find that this varies from about forty years in African, South American, and Asiatic societies—and even in some European ones east of the Iron Curtain—to something like seventy years in societies west of the Iron Curtain and in our United States. The gap is attributed to a "standard of living" which itself is an effect whereof the cause is the democratic organization and use of power in order to produce an ever greater and more varied abundance of food, clothing, shelter, playthings, work-tools, medicines, and esthetic, religious, and scientific valuables, all being orchestrated into a style of life, which here is called "the American Way," and is envisioned as "the American Dream."

Millions of American dreamers are not yet upon this way and live almost as badly off as the multitudes of Asia, Africa, South America and Eastern Europe. But the national effort to get them set upon the way is persistent, and becomes, with time, more and more successful. For youth gets the chance of growing into maturity and old age by way of an education that can enable it to render its latter days richer and freer than its earlier. And this is the case with groups within the society as it is with their members. It holds for them jointly and severally—communities as well as families, cities as well as communities, states and nations as well as cities, the United Nations as well as the member nations. In spite of the bloody conflicts and rivalries of the peoples of the earth, their global orchestration does make headway in that the poor and ignorant among them are moved to emulate the educated and richer and are impelled to learn how knowledge is power and how this power can be used to achieve a freer and more abundant life for themselves and their posterity. The education which teaches this is now declared every person's unalienable right.

Let us for a moment set this knowledge which, as power, converts the facts of nature into the resources of man for living more freely, safely and abundantly while in the natural world, beside the knowledge which is power to get him out of this world when he dies, into an other, a superior nonnatural world. St. Paul called the first "wisdom of the world" and declared it to be "foolishness with God, who taketh the wise in their own craftiness" (Corinthians, 4). He opposed to it the Wisdom of God which he declared was foolishness with the worldly wise. He may be said to have, in a sense, confirmed the observation of Ecclesiastes, "In much wisdom is much grief and he that increaseth knowledge increaseth sorrow" (I, 18). If Lord Acton is right, and, as he says, power corrupts, absolute power corrupts absolutely, then the replacement and extension of manpower by the knowledge which is power could be exposed as the most corrupting development of human history; then only the incorruptible power which is the wisdom of God can save mankind from the grief, the suffering, and the corruption caused by the knowledge which is the dy-

namic of human power in this vale of tears. The maxim, "if ignorance is bliss, 'tis folly to be wise" may express the concentrated
wisdom of the ages.

But this is no longer the conclusion of unenlightened any
more than of enlightened humans. Very many of those who have
taken teaching the wisdom of God for their vocation have so
compenetrated it with the knowledge which Bacon first called
power, that the two can be distinguished from one another only
with very great difficulty, and not too successfully. The consensus is worldwide that the sciences of man and nature are the most
reliable, the most fruitful substance of human, as against man,
power to render human experience freer, safer and more abundant. To qualify this power as black, white, yellow, red, or in any
other such way, adds nothing to it and takes nothing from it. The
adjectives in no way enhance or minimize an individual's or a
group's capacity to learn and to use what they learn in order to
advance toward freer, safer, fuller life. As employed, the adjectives signify merely possession or lack. To say "Black Power" is
to declare a lack and to proclaim a will to make good this lack.

In so far as power is knowledge, the will to power must be
first of all a will to knowledge. Knowledge can be gained by
learning it by oneself or by learning from those who already have
it. The former is the hardest, the slowest of hard and slow ways,
practically impossible on our harried earth. The latter is the mode
of education everywhere on the globe. In practice, it is the act of
equalizing knowledge by sharing it; teaching is the sharing of
knowledge, and the sharer must have the wherewithal to share. I
know of no other way of equalizing knowledge. When a Stokely
Carmichael, advocating Black Power, threatens: "When you talk
of Black Power you talk of building a movement that will smash
everything Western civilization has created," he threatens the destruction of all that distinguishes human power from the power of
animal man. Unless Black Power has already shared and made its
own "everything Western civilization has created" it can only
avert from human power to the mere man-power of ignorance
and poverty it purports to fight against. If, on the other hand,
Black Power has already shared by learning the human power of

Western civilization, it can only perpetuate and advance it. If Black Power intends more and better power for Negro Americans or Negro Africans, it must diversify, and add to, what it already has. It must will to know as much and as well as those already possessing the knowledge which is power and must strive to learn more and master it more successfully. Striving to share equally, its word to Western civilization could well be: "Anything you can do, I can do better." I doubt, if in the nature of things, there is another way.

For, even if teaching could be successfully coerced, learning cannot be, though the teacher practice brainwashing. Communication between teacher and learner is authentic education when both engage in it with concerned goodwill—the one to share what he already has, the other to receive possession of what he has not yet, each aware of the other as a member of a team playing to reach a common goal—the learner's attainment of a specific power. If he does not bring to the teacher an open heart, open eyes and ears and willing hands, how much of what the teacher imparts can the learner absorb and digest into himself? And if the teacher doesn't bring to the learner a warm-hearted readiness to give, patience and perseverance in giving, how much can he effectively impart? It is true that humans do learn many things from experience as animals do, by the trials and errors of instinctive transactions like breathing or feeding. But learning is human in virtue of the added factor of sharing through communication. This is paramount. Not to share is to deny another human his unalienable human right. And without power, rights are empty phrases whose meaning power-holders everywhere tend to disregard, since everywhere power without rights tends, as Lord Acton observed, to corrupt into irresponsible and totalitarian tyranny. Uncontained by rights, power is merely the blind, destructive, animal energy of the hairless ape which other animals manifest only when they are panicked by pain or fear or rage. It is the power of mob-violence, of rioters, which can create nothing but can destroy everything unless contained and redirected. Rights and laws are the human containers. Their role in human relations suggests the role of machines and computers in the man-

agement of non-human things. Humanly, power gets brought together with rights and laws in such a way that the capacity for
learning which is the differentia of the human, achieves such an
insight into the nature and uses of things that the learner feels
what he has learned as part and parcel of his selfhood.

So complete a digestion and assimilation of knowledge does
not occur as often as it might, although it is commoner than we
think. No matter what Descartes or the existentialists imagine, we
learn very little from our awareness and study of our segregated
selves: most of what we are aware of has been communicated to
us from outside. The persons and places and forms "out there"
both are and provide the subject matter of our studies. They
compound into the configurations of our day-to-day experiences,
the forms and events of the aggregate society without boundaries
which environs our ongoing strivings to live on. They carry "atmosphere," they convey the "climate of opinion" as it changes.
Black Power will establish itself as a lasting and stable organization of interest among the others in our democratic society, only
as it participates in these studies, with due regard to these contexts. Else it will be a passing tornado blowing out and blowing
up in violence and destruction, with only ruin behind.

Nothing in the history of any society's progress is more utopian a fantasy than the oft-recurring belief that progress follows
razing what has already been built and starting afresh in a vac-
uum. It is a fantasy about society which repeats this about individuals: that human persons can destroy their past and not destroy themselves; that they can grow new selves on no ground,
from no roots, and no nourishment which only the past can provide. They cannot. A person's past is all he is: his entire past,
remembered and unremembered, is all he becomes in his career as
man. His identity consists in the present changing of the past he is
into the past he keeps becoming as, experience after experience,
he adds what he is not yet. Fulfilling his aspirations, becoming
later what he presently imagines and desires to become, makes up
his career as man. He diversifies his past with the future he joins
to it, and so forms his identity. His whole career is a progression
and the progression is a learning, as the cliché, living is learning,
learning is living, sums life up. Progression becomes education

whenever another human teaches the learner what he learns. So, again, communication between teacher and learner is almost the all of education.

In sum, wherever we turn, we find education to be the *sine qua non* of human, vis-à-vis man-power, horsepower, and every other form of primitive power, including divine power. This primitive power the sciences examine, disclose, define, control and use in order to satisfy human needs and to realize human ideals. The religions were earlier means to these ends. Read, for instance, the Prophet Isaiah, comforting his people, way back about 842 B.C.E. He describes an existence which is still normal in most of the Middle East, and pledges that it shall be corrected, as follows:

> The poor and needy seek water and there is none.
> And their tongue faileth for thirst;
> I, the Lord, will answer them, I the God of Israel
>   will not forsake them.
> I will make the wilderness a pool of water,
> And the dry lands springs of water.
> I will plant in the wilderness the cedar, the acacia tree,
> And the myrtle, and the oil tree:
> I will set in the desert the cypress, the plane tree,
>   and the laurel together.
> That they may see, and know,
> And consider, and understand together
> That the hand of the Lord hath done this,
> And the Holy One of Israel created it.

Somehow this promised future never came; the promise was never kept. The history of that little, barren landbridge between Africa, Asia and Europe called the land of Israel is an item of man's struggle to change the desert of his thirst and hunger into a well-watered garden land producing abundantly to satisfy both, and in the land of Israel failing still, while the Lord's chosen people also heard the prophetic invocations of the past (Isaiah, 42: 6, 8) to strengthen them against their anxieties over the present and fears of the future:

> I, the Lord have called thee in righteousness.
> And have taken hold of thy hand.
> And kept thee, and set thee for a covenant of the people.

For a light of the nations,
To open the blind eyes,
To bring out the prisoners from the dungeon.
And them that sit in the darkness of the prison-house.

And here again is the ideal future for the Lord's chosen, not only, but for all mankind, as the prophet Micah envisions it (Micah 4:1–7, especially verses 1–4):

It shall come to pass in the latter days, that the mountain of the house of the Lord shall be established as the highest of mountains, and shall be raised up above the hills; and peoples shall flow to it, and many nations shall come and say: Come, let us go up to the mountain of the Lord, to the house of the God of Jacob, that he may teach us his ways and we may walk in his paths. For out of Zion shall go forth the Law, and the Word of the Lord, from Jerusalem. He shall judge between many peoples, and shall decide for strong nations afar off; and they shall beat their swords into plowshares and their spears into pruning-hooks. Nation shall not lift up sword against nation, neither shall they learn war any more: but they shall sit every man under his vine and under his fig tree, and none shall make them afraid: for the mouth of the Lord of hosts has spoken. For all the peoples walk each in the name of its god, but we will walk in the name of the Lord our God forever and ever.

And is not this vision still the vision of the future which has never yet come to change the past, to say nothing of destroying it? In all of the vision's diversifications—political, poetic, philosophical—it continues a Utopian aspiration, compensating, with an image designing a world which is not yet, for the travail and tragedy of the world which continues too much as it was. Insofar as vision comes to event at all, reliance on divine providence is first supplanted, then replaced by reliance on the knowledge which is human power. Thus, most of today's children of Israel abandon waiting for the Lord to do it and strive to do it themselves. In order to secure water, to produce food, to achieve health, freedom, safety and beauty, they seek the kind of education which shall teach them the ways and works of nature and how to use them as a means to the survival and growth of man. And that their education may succeed, they neither suppress nor propose to abolish their heritage from the past—is this not their human *haecceitas?*—but to orchestrate it into the future they are creating to join to it. Thus they may, and the Arabs of Israel together with them, be said to be fulfilling the promise the Lord has not fulfilled.

Would you not agree that there is, in this instance of knowledge as power, something worth examining for those of us who feel a concern for the development and success of Black Power here at home or anywhere in the world? When we say "Black Power" we have in mind millions of fellow-citizens who have been denied access to the knowledge which is power creatively, who have thus been starved in soul and disabled from achieving their optimum as human persons, as members of a society of true believers in articles of faith set forth by the Declaration of Independence—and constituting what Theodore Parker has called *The American Idea.* The world of this *Idea* is a world of individuals all of whom are different from each other but are equal *as* different, and are, as different, equally endowed with unalienable rights of which the rights to life, liberty, and the pursuit of happiness are among the more paramount. In such a world, government can but work as a means with which the people provide themselves "in order to secure these rights." Government's role is to insure everybody against the alienation of his rights by anybody, including government, and to restore them to equality where alienation of the unalienable is believed to be at work.

What, then, in the frame of reference of the American Idea, the only frame on which it can rely for opportunity, is the shape of the future for Black Power? Is it not education? Is it not to keep learning and using the knowledge which is power over ignorance, poverty, disease, ugliness, and whatever other weaknesses beset human life, and which brings the self-assurance and the serenity of soul which the social order based on equal liberty generates and nourishes? Education so designed and so at work is equalization in power. If the non-blacks are today more powerful than the blacks it is because they, almost alone, cultivate the knowledge which is power. It is from them who have that the have-nots must learn, if they honestly aim to attain the equality in right which the American Idea declares their birthright. As the record throughout the nation discloses, all patriots loyal to the Idea have shown a working concern for the equalization in power of all

Americans, whatever their derivation, and particularly now the Negro-Americans, by means of education. Indeed, education as equalization is at last a world-wide claim which the Universal Declaration of Human Rights asserts for all humans everywhere. But as a long, by comparison unstinting, nation-wide endeavor, education as equalization in the United States has no parallel. In our unusually free (Yes, with all its prohibitions, barriers, and coercions, free) and our unusually prosperous (Yes, with all its poor and ignorant and sick, man for man and job for job, prosperous) country, there is no boundary to the gains in power an individual or a group may achieve by means of education, and no barrier to the education. As the Lord, speaking with the voice of his prophet said of himself, *"Not by force, not by might, but by my spirit."* And the chalice of the spirit can be nothing else than the education of the peoples which—John Milton said it—frees them "to perform justly, skillfully, and thoughtfully all the offices both public and private, of peace and war," and so freeing them, instills them with the self-respect he defines as "the pious and just honoring of ourselves." To what greater distinction could Black Power aspire, what nobler goal could it aim at, what more reliable means could it work with to attain its goals?

9 | What Should Be the Relation of Morals to Law?

I am bothered, in reflecting upon this question, by the word "should." Mostly, people use it when they are dissatisfied with things-as-they-are, and want them changed. Sometimes the change is conceived as necessitated by an external force, sometimes as demanded by an inward desire. In the former case, people are apt to say it "ought" to be; in the latter, that they "had rather," that they "had liefer," it be. They use "should" in either sense, and sometimes in both at once. They make it signify obligation and duty, they make it signify desire, and they make it signify the harmony of duty and desire.

Now, as I read the record, the relations between law, ethics and morals are many, varied and inconsistent; and the law, ethics and morals between which these relations come and go are also plural and diverse. A relation that some people in some places might regard as necessary or desirable or both might be regarded by others in the same place as a condition to be changed. A rela-

tion that might be entirely satisfactory in one region or one culture might be judged as the opposite in others. What moral or
legal writ runs where depends in any actual situation upon people,
their personal histories, hopes, fears, loves, hates, culture, training,
insight and courage. Although the maxim exalts "government of
laws" and deprecates "government of men," the fact is indefeasible that laws define ways of behaving toward one another for
men, that they either express and sustain men's attitudes and
habits, or repress and work to alter them. "Law" usually denotes
written documents, such as constitutions, statutes, ordinances,
codes, decrees, digests and the like; it suggests courthouses, police
stations, jails, law schools and law offices. But it does not equally
suggest that these are tools and agencies by means of which people called lawmakers, lawyers, judges, juries, sheriffs, bailiffs, con-
stables and policemen, come into certain relations with one another and with members of the residual public. It does not suggest
the functionaries who administer and enforce the laws, nor the
public who obey, defy or disregard them. "Law" does not suggest
that its life does not inhere in what it prescribes or forbids, but in
the ability of the few men and women called "officers of the law"
to enforce, and in the willingness of the many men and women to
obey. "Law" does not suggest that both ability to enforce and
willingness to obey are aspects of a social atmosphere whence the
individuals, who are born into it and grow up in it, maintaining
and altering it, draw the works and ways with thoughts and
things that they weave into the singularities of their personal histories. If we mean by morals these altering constellations of works
and ways, in their patterned concreteness of ongoing change, then
the relations of morals and laws are dynamic and inward; the two
are members of one another as parts of an organism are members
of one another. The morality prevailing determines the efficacy
of the law; the administration of the law confirms the morality
prevailing. Every region of the world provides characteristic instances of this relationship: Catholic countries, in laws affecting
Protestants and other variants; Islamic countries, in laws affecting
non-Islamic communities; countries dominated by whites like
South Africa and our own Southern states, in laws affecting Negroes.

Every so often some phase of the process of change in morals, either inwardly initiated, or as response to outer influences, will evoke the promulgation of laws designed to arrest or prevent the change. Again, men of good will, holding that change cannot be prevented, conceding that it is desirable or even necessary, will insist that laws cannot change morals, and that either a policy solely of moral laissez faire or of moral education must be depended upon to lead to the general consent on which observance of the law depends. Consciously or unconsciously they assume that laws, being rules for future conduct, look back to and consummate past tradition, whether as folkways and mores, or as covenants or conventions of belief and practice. So conceived, laws signalize the unity of community; they are the terms of union in communion, the spirit and power of peoples belonging together, and their use is to serve as conservators or preservers of this spirit and power. Hence, it is the height of unwisdom wilfully to tamper with them. So long as they are on the books, they should be obeyed. Morally, no one is above the law, however bad the law may be.

This view of what should be the relation of law to morals has a certain kinship with that which Plato assigns to Socrates, in his dialogue, *Crito*. Socrates, it will be remembered, has been condemned to death. His friends have arranged for his escape, and Crito has been sent to the prison to take the old philosopher to safety and freedom. Socrates declines to be rescued. He has, he indicates to his young friend, been sentenced to death under due process of the law. The sentence is unjust and not in accord with the facts, but it has been lawfully rendered. It is a judgment which the whole society passes upon a part for the sake of its own freedom and safety as a whole, and its laws are the very life of this wholeness. An individual is at once the "child and slave" of the society he was born into and in which he grows up and grows old. He is the creation of this society and always under its authority. The virtue of a citizen is the virtue of a soldier. It involves accepting suffering and death at the hands of this higher authority, "or he must change their views of what is just." Failing to change their views he should submit to them; otherwise, he will be "breaking covenants and agreements" and contribute to destroying the State. Better is it for him as an individual to suffer evil than to do evil, and by suffering, "fulfill the will of God."

A modern version of the old Sophist's stand is the formula, "my country, may she ever be right, but right or wrong, my country." This is its "republican" form. Its monarchical equivalent is: "The King can do no wrong," *king* standing here, of course, not for the person who discharges the function of lawgiver, but for the functioning law itself. It expresses the intention of the maxim attributed to Louis XIV, *L'état c'est moi*, when monarchical government is itself conceived as a government of laws, not of men. In the *Crito*, Socrates implies that all government, to be government at all, must be of laws and not of men, and that the injustice they happen to do is a contingency of the justice they must maintain. Implicit in the idea is the belief that individuals are and can be nothing on their own account; that they receive from the society in which they live and move and have their being all they are, all they possess, all they achieve; that they live and grow by its grace, under its authority; that whatever personal dignity and worth they embody are secondary and derivative, and accrue to individuals as grants and privileges. The idea is that the society or the State is equally the substance, the seat and the standard of value—the end of ends to which individuals are but means; and that the conservation and advancement of this social end justify the unjust means of unmerited punishment, even unto death, of each and every individual.

Western history records many reformulations of this Platonic ethics of law. These, like Hobbes' *Leviathan*, are regularly both authoritarian and totalitarian. Roman Catholic sacerdotalism provides a traditional version of it; Hitler's nazi fascism and Mussolini's fascist corporationism, and Stalin's Marxist communazism, with their variants in Asia and Africa, provide versions which challenge the anxious attention of freedom-loving people everywhere in today's world. That most of them begin by a greater or lesser violent overturn of the moral order prevailing, that they impose a code of ethics and incarnate it in laws whose entire sanction is at first outer force and not inner faith, has little influence on this ethic of the laws, which ultimately comes down in Church and State alike, to Mussolini's maxim, *credere, obedire, combattere*.

Against this venerable ethic, which power-holders of societies have perennially fought to impose as law and to develop as social institutions and personal habits of belief and action, we may set another in fundamental respects its opposite. This other expresses the original nature of *Homo sapiens*. It develops, diversifies and perfects his native disposition, which is, always and everywhere, to behave in such a way as to preserve the integrity and mobility of his independent being, and to fight off total incorporation in any group and total subordination to any authority: to be let alone. As Mr. Justice Brandeis saw it, the laws of a free society affirm and safeguard this disposition; he called it "the right to be let alone—the most comprehensive of rights and the right most valued by civilized men." [1]

The Christian view of human nature, prior to the Protestant Reformation, had consistently condemned this disposition as the substance of evil. It had equated original nature with original sin and had urged that the moral virtues, ultimately deriving from the "love" of a man for his fellow man, could be only nonnatural acquisitions dependent on divine grace and resting on obedience to God's revealed commandments and that the charismatic powers of Church and State interpret, specify and implement these commandments by means of canon and civil law. In this view, virtue and goodness could not be a ripening of inborn propensities responsive to the impacts of the human scene and the instruction of the elders. But, from the Protestant Reformation on, the belief spread that they could be. The Reformation idea of the autonomy and integrity of the private conscience developed into the understanding that original nature was original virtue as well as original sin and that the corruption of the former was the work of the authoritarian powers of Church and State. Enlightened man came to believe that governments, *i.e.*, social organizations and their laws, are means only, never ends, and that the indefeasibly different individuals united into such organizations are, as

[1] Mr. Justice Brandeis, dissenting, in Olmstead v. United States, 277 U.S. 438, 478 (1928).

Immanuel Kant emphasized, always ends and never means, and that law should impattern their equal safety and freedom.

This ethic became the gospel of a new dispensation. In the form of our American Declaration of Independence it took on the role of an ethic of social change and became the practical initiation of the Democratic Revolution. Free men have been working and fighting for its global consummation ever since. Between the Declaration of Independence, to whose support our founding fathers pledged their lives, their liberty and their sacred honor, and the Universal Declaration of Human Rights, to whose realization the spokesmen of all the free peoples of the world committed themselves, there is a stretch of 172 years. They are years of ever-expanding struggle to transpose profession into performance, moral principle into legal practice, to devise and to perfect laws which should be the most efficacious means to the collective attainment of the distributive ends of life, liberty and the pursuit of happiness that are the equal and unalienable rights of unlike and unequal persons. The proposition that these rights are ends innate to each and every human being and that governments are means to secure these ends has been again and again invoked in every walk of life as a fighting faith to oppose to its prevailing opposite of authoritarianism and totalitarianism. There is no free society whose constitution, whether written or unwritten, is not an arrangement of law designed to realize this faith in works, a means to achieve this end. The Constitution of the United States was explicitly devised as such a means, and the rules of its alteration and amendments, so that it might the better serve its ends, are explicitly laid down. The ends are stated in the Preamble: ". . . to form a more perfect Union, establish Justice, insure domestic Tranquility, provide for the common defence, promote the general Welfare, and secure the Blessings of Liberty to ourselves and Posterity. . . ." They are equally the ends of all the people, all different in ethnic derivation, sex, religion, occupation, possessions, age and powers; and the people's amendments of the Constitution and the powers of government to make laws and enforce them are alike directed to the realization of these ends.

That their realization is always struggle, not infrequently

bloody and bitter struggle, is a historic truism. Continuously in this struggle the opponents endeavor to give the old formulations of the Constitution new meanings suited to the region, the time, the climate of opinion, the interests and perhaps the consciences of the combatants. During the struggle over slavery, the private conscience tended to overrule all laws; the abolitionists appealing to the basic ethic of democracy which they called "the higher law," the secessionists identifying the enslavement of men with the rights of states, Abraham Lincoln insisting on the inviolability of the Union without or with slavery, and thinking emancipation as a means to preserve the Union as well as thinking it a means to realize the equal liberty of all men as an end in itself. Others, again, when they believe that the laws are prospering their own interest and that the administration of them confirms their prosperity, will develop a fanaticism about "the preservation of law and order" and will forget their ends in their pursuit of means. They will transpose the social tool into a personal idol, regardless of consequences to other interests and to their own.

All the forces in play have their to me most signal current exemplification in the struggle over civil rights and FEPC and over the separation of Church and State and its bearing on the curricula of the nation's schools and the nation's arts and sciences. These are issues of the greatest ethical import. Their resolution, not by force, not by might, but according to the spirit of the laws, involves continuous reconsideration of the Bill of Rights, of the Thirteenth, Fourteenth and Fifteenth Amendments, and determination of their meanings by the Supreme Court. This determination, with its divisions, may appear to be an operation of legal semantics. But it is never what it appears to be. Underlying the Court's unequal and diverse majorities, and its diverse and unequal minorities, is the personal history, the experience, the knowledge, and ultimately the ethical disposition of each justice acting and reacting with all the others. In the end, thus, as Mr. Justice Hughes pointed out, the Constitution is what the judges say it is, and what the judges say it is depends in the last resort on whether their ethic is an ethic of freedom or an ethic of authority. Under an ethic of freedom the meaning of the law is always subject to

revision. But whatever the judges say, the saying becomes the occasion's rule and road of social change on which even mutually
inimical interests may move without resort to force or fraud.
That in their desire to avert or facilitate social change they often
do so resort is of course but another truism to which the power
granted the State to enforce the law testifies. This power is, however, at the opposite pole of the dictatorial power of authoritarian
government in totalitarian societies, with its presumption of infal-
libility.

I may now venture my answer to the question: What
"should" be the relation of morals to "law"?

My preference is for the ethic of freedom whose principles
are stated in the Declaration of Independence and the Universal
Declaration of Human Rights. Where the morality prevailing is
unfriendly to this ethic, I believe that law should be so formulated
and implemented as to convert it to friendliness. Where the
morality prevailing is consistent with this ethic, I believe that law
should be so framed as to extend and confirm it. The task is universal and endemic. To many it seems hopeless. They see a totalitarian society with an authoritarian ethic and a corpus juris of
decrees pressing for mastery of all the peoples of the globe. They
see in relatively free societies new strengthenings of traditional
authoritarianism. They see the United Nations paralyzed and the
laws of nations unenforceable except by preponderant force.
They see violence and warfare regionally a fact and globally imminent. They feel anxious and at a loss. They speak of our age as
an "age of anxiety." But their fears have made them blind to the
positive gains of the ethic of freedom, and the positive rallying to
it everywhere in the world. In the hearts of men the totalitarian
ethic finds no response. It is always imposed from without, not
assented to from within. Those who live under it live as subjects
under fear, not as citizens in freedom. Its strength is the strength
of force and fraud, not of covenant. Expose the deception, confront the force with equal and greater force, and the totalitarian
whole disintegrates and the authoritarian ethic collapses.

On the record of the past century and three-quarters, the
ethic of freedom prevails where men who are different from each

other join together as equals in the fighting faith which commits their lives, their fortunes and their sacred honors to its support— its support in and through the laws being at once the means and ends of their personal survival and growth as free men.

10 "E Pluribus Unum" and the Cultures of Democracy

There is an issue of human relations which is as old as mankind and as inveterate as thought. Philosophers call it "the problem of the One and the Many" and find it also the basic problem of existence. Humanly, however, it is the problem of how people who are different from each other shall live together with each other. It is the critical problem of each personal life, of each race, sect, sex, occupational group, political party, sovereign state, and religious establishment.

The history of mankind indicates two major ways of solving this problem, ways that recur, with variations, in philosophy and the other arts and sciences as well as in more "practical" affairs.

The first and by far the older and more prevalent way is to deny all rights to the *different*. Some primitives utterly extirpate the different; others make them one with themselves by eating them; others by attaching their heads or scalps to their own persons or possessions; still others by degrading the different to slav-

124

ery—in Aristotle's words, to the status of a tool with life in it. More advanced societies have employed enslavement more than slaughter, though they have always countered disobedience or nonconformity with the threat of death. Their elite have been conquerors; their ideal has been total unity achieved by warfare and imposed by victory, a unity in which every part draws its existence, its meaning, and its value from the one absolute, indivisible sovereign whole. Under this unity, that only can be true which the sovereign says is true—the different is heresy, error, or infidelity; that only can be right which the sovereign says is right —the different is immorality, sin, or treason. Under its doctrine and discipline, to be different is to be evil and to merit either punishment or destruction.

Since all nature breeds and multiplies differences, differences come into existence willy-nilly—different species, different peoples, different communities with different economies, different faiths, different cultures, and different ways of life and living. The mere existence of these differents is a denial of the claims and a challenge to the rule of those who speak on behalf of a One, sole, exclusive, sovereign authority. Such an authority, consequently, be it political, ecclesiastical, economic, or what have you, is compelled in the nature of things to spend much of its force in suppressing or destroying the different, especially that which makes rival claims to unique sovereignty. As the enemy of difference, such authority is also the enemy of freedom, since freedom lives and moves and has its being in the right to be different. It wages a permanent war against freedom.

The doctrine and discipline of the Nazis and the Japanese are today's most sadistocratic embodiment of this warfare against freedom, this undertaking of those who would impose their One to destroy or to enslave those who acknowledge and respect the equal liberty of the Many.

The second way of resolving the problem of the One and the Many starts in such acknowledgment and respect. We call it the democratic way. Its device is *e pluribus unum*. Its doctrine is stated by the Declaration of Independence, its discipline by the Constitution. The living faith that sustains doctrine and discipline does not require the submergence or subordination of the different; it requires the coöperation or teamplay of the different on equal terms. The unity of the democratic way is a *union* that emerges from and consists in this teamplay. It takes form as a free association, and it rules not as a sovereign imposing its authority from without and above, but as a servant receiving its authority from within and beneath. Living, in such a federal union, is characterized by the fact that no relation in it is rigid, fixed, compulsive. Individuals and associations of individuals, each different from the others, live together with the others in such a way that all may enjoy the freest possible movement, the greatest possible initiative. They form an *open* society, in which hindrances to free communications are at a minimum, and the process of free communication on all levels—economic, religious, aesthetic, scientific, and political—constitutes the bond of union between the different communicants.

An educated man is distinguished from an ignoramus, a tolerant man from an intolerant, a man of culture from a barbarian, and a free man from a servile one by his desire for and training in free communication with the different. Among free men, the entire purpose of education is mastery of the means and methods of free communication. Such a mastery is, and always has been, culture; and it measures any person's readiness to live and to grow in a civilization that is naturally a cultural pluralism and that takes the fact of this pluralism as the basic material of its cultural ideal.

It is for the survival of such a civilization of cultural pluralism as fact and as ideal that we and our allies are today at war. As the United States of America are many communities of peoples bound to each other by free communication into one nation; as the British Commonwealth of Nations are many peoples, the strength of whose bond is measured by the freedom of their association, so are the United Nations. Yellow men, black men, brown men, and red men, as well as white; Confucians, Buddhists, Mohammedans, Parsees, Sikhs, and Bahais and countless other faiths and cultures as well as Judaist, Catholic, and Protestant are joined together as equal soldiers in the war to vindicate the freedom of their manyness against the servitude of the Japanazi oneness. They uphold the spiritual abundance of their cultural pluralism against the spiritual scarcity of the foe's monist *Kultur*. They advance the spontaneous orchestration of the freely coöperating Many against the servile coördination of the foe's regimented One; they pit the strength of the teamplay of a Federal Union against the changing force of a sovereign unity.

Cultural pluralism thus defines both the material and the spiritual intent of the four freedoms. It is both the means and the goal of a way of life for whose survival and growth American history has been an unceasing struggle. Today it embodies the form of those freedoms that are the hope of all the world.

11 | Alain Locke and Cultural Pluralism

Please don't be disturbed by this list of now second-hand books that Dr. Krikorian has provided for you. I am not as formidable as that sounds. I am simply concerned, as we all must be in these times of ours, about the meaning and the future of freedom, alike as a philosophical conception and as a working idea.

The expression "cultural pluralism" must now be familiar to all of you. It has figured in the public prints. It has come to denote one of the alternatives of foreign policy for our State Department. Even members of the Security Council and the General Staff are reported as talking about the importance of the Bill of Rights and the intercultural relations which the Bill of Rights implies as against those implied by totalitarian creeds. It is not possible to implement any of the propositions of our American Bill or of the Universal Declaration of Human Rights of the United Nations without assuming the primacy and the irreducible plurality of the cultures of mankind and their impact on one another.

As an expression in the American language "cultural pluralism" is about 50 years old. I used it first around 1906 or 1907 when Alain Locke was in a section of a class at Harvard where I served as assistant to Mr. George Santayana. It has taken these two generations for the term to come into more general use and to figure in philosophical discourse in this country. Locke, you may remember, refers in one of his philosophical essays to a book by F. C. S. Northrop of Yale, entitled "The Meeting of East and West," and indeed since the First World War the expression has recurred in public discussion more and more frequently and more diversely.

In my mind, here is what it fundamentally signifies: first, a concept that social science and social philosophy can and do employ as a working hypothesis concerning human nature and human relations; second, an ethical ideal—an article of faith which challenges certain prevailing philosophical conceptions about both. Those conceptions are fundamentally monistic. There persists in the sciences of man and nature and in philosophies as they have developed in our country, a disposition to assert and somehow to establish the primacy of totalitarian unity at the beginning, and its supremacy in the consummation, of all existence. It is, of course, conceded that multitude and variety seem pervasive, always and everywhere. But it is denied that they are real. It is the One that is real, not the Many—whether we regard many things or many men. Men come and go but Man goes on forever, and it is in their eternal and universal Manhood that all men are brothers. That this brotherhood involves the blood rivalry of Cain and Abel perhaps much more commonly than the relationship between David and Jonathan seems not to affect this monist creed, nor the cliché regarding the fatherhood of God and the brotherhood of Man, which is one of its commoner expressions. A better word for what is intended by "brotherhood" is the word "friendship." For this word carries no implication of an identical beginning and common end that are to be attributed to the event that two persons or two peoples or a thousand peoples who are different from each other and must perforce live together with each other, seek such ways of togetherness as shall be ways of peace and freedom.

Now, the expression "cultural pluralism" is intended to signify this endeavor toward friendship by people who are different from each other but who, as different, hold themselves equal to each other. By "equal" we commonly mean "similar" or "identical." "Cultural pluralism," however, intends by "equal" also parity of the unequal, equality of the unlike, not only of the like or the same. It postulates that individuality is indefeasible, that differences are primary, and that consequently human beings have an indefeasible right to their differences and should not be penalized for their differences, however they may be constituted, whatever they may consist in: color, faith, sex, occupation, possessions, or what have you. On the record, nevertheless, human beings continually penalize one another for their differences. This is how they exemplify the brotherhood of man and the fatherhood of God; how the South Africans are brothers to their dark-skinned victims, the Chinese to the Koreans, the Arabs to the Israelis, and the Russians to non-Communist mankind. Each demands of his sibling, "Agree with me, be my brother—or else! And so that you may become completely a brother, you must offer up your own different being to be digested into identification with mine. You must replace your purposes with mine, your ways and means with mine. Unless you do this you refuse brotherhood." Contrast this requirement with the requirement of friendship, which says to the other fellow not "Be my brother" but *"Be my friend.* I am different from you. You are different from me. The basis of our communion is our difference. Let us exchange the fruits of our differences so that each may enrich the other with what the other is not or has not in himself. In what else are we important to one another, what else can we pool and share if not our differences?" The valuations here postulated should be obvious. If for example, in coming here today, we had expected merely a repetition of what we already know and feel, it is unlikely that even our reverence to a notable friend and beautiful character would have brought us. We expect something somehow still unknown and unpossessed. We do not care to seek what we already sufficiently have. We want what we don't yet have. This is how we achieve spiritual abundance, which consists in the free and friendly barter of different things and thoughts and neighborly relations. It lives in untrammeled communication between the different on all levels. It signalizes the idea of civilization that the expression "cultural pluralism" denotes.

Now this is what Alain Locke envisioned from the time that he became reconciled to himself. He became a cultural pluralist. It took him some time.

In 1935 Sidney Hook and I got out a collection of essays by younger United States philosophers entitled, *American Philosophy Today and Tomorrow*. Alain Locke contributed to this collection a paper on the theme, "Values and Imperatives." Each contributor accompanied his essay with a short autobiographical note. I will read you Locke's note which, I suspect, is not as familiar to his friends as it should be, and then ask what it postulates *en philosophe*. How did the author get this way? How came Locke —a proud and sensitive man who was penalized by "whites" for his darker skin, in matters of spirit an incidental difference—to give up the idea of equality as identification, as sameness with whites, and to urge equality as parity in and of his difference from the whites; hence to see the human enterprise as free, friendly, creative intercommunication between differents and their reciprocal enrichment thereby?

> I should like to claim [he wrote] as life-motto the good Greek principle,—*"Nothing in excess,"* but I have probably worn instead as the badge of circumstance,—*"All things with a reservation."* Philadelphia, with her birthright of provincialism flavored by urbanity and her petty bourgeois psyche with the Tory slant, at the start set the key of paradox; circumstance compounded it by decreeing me as a Negro a dubious and doubting sort of American and by reason of the racial inheritance making me more of a pagan than a Puritan, more of a humanist than a pragmatist.
>
> Verily paradox has followed me the rest of my days: at Harvard, clinging to the genteel tradition of Palmer, Royce and Münsterberg, yet attracted by the disillusion of Santayana and the radical protest of James: again in 1916 I returned to work under Royce but was destined to take my doctorate in Value Theory under Perry. At Oxford, once more intrigued by the twilight of aestheticism but dimly aware of the new realism of the Austrian philosophy of value; socially Anglophile, but because of race loyalty, strenuously anti-imperialist; universalist in religion, internationalist and pacifist in world-view, but forced by a sense of simple justice to approve of the militant counter-nationalisms of

Zionism, Young Turkey, Young Egypt, Young India, and with reservations even Garveyism and current-day 'Nippon over Asia.' Finally a cultural cosmopolitan, but perforce an advocate of cultural racialism as a defensive counter-move for the American Negro, and accordingly more of a philosophical mid-wife to a generation of younger Negro poets, writers, artists than a professional philosopher.

Small wonder, then, with this psychograph, that I project my personal history into its inevitable rationalization as cultural pluralism and value relativism, with a not too orthodox reaction to the American way of life.

Locke presents himself here with the passions and powers of his individuality. His singularity is evident, and he gives hints of his idiosyncrasy. But he accepted neither, although he couldn't reject them. He felt, in sense and intellect, a human being the same as other human beings, especially white ones who denied the sameness. He knew that in his ideals, his intentions, and his works and ways he was not inferior, nor otherwise different from those people who held themselves to be better than he was and there were intervals—one was certainly his undergraduate days at Harvard—when he did not appear to live under any penalty for his difference. He seems not to have in Philadelphia. I know that at Oxford—I was there at the time—he was penalized. There were among the Rhodes scholars at Oxford gentlemen from Dixie who could not possibly associate with Negroes. They could not possibly attend the Thanksgiving dinner celebrated by Americans if a Negro was to be there. So although students from elsewhere in the United States outnumbered the gentlemen from Dixie, Locke was not invited, and one or two other persons, authentically Americans, refused in consequence to attend. You might say it was a dinner of inauthentic Americans. Now, the impact of that kind of experience left scars. The more so in a philosophic spirit. For the dominant trend among philosophers is always to prove unity and to work at unifications—to assert *one* humanity, *one* universe, *one* system of values and ideals which somehow is coërcive of the many and somehow argues away the actualities of penalization for one's being oneself into unimportant appearances, without in any way relieving the feelings of dehumanization, the pain and the suffering; and without lessening the desire never again to expose oneself to them. There were times that year when Locke thought never to return to the United States. In fact, he deeply wanted not to. He was at ease in Europe. The penalties for "color," especially in France and on the continent, were not apparent. They were not as apparent in England as they are today. But however or wherever the penalties were laid, Locke felt he could not expose himself to their indignities. As a human being with an individuality of his own, he knew that no commitment or obligation could be laid on him heavier than anybody else's, and that the necessities of vindicating his integrity and realizing his own potentialities in his own way had the first claim and the last.

It took him some time to find his way to that acquiescence in unalienable right to his difference, which became the core of his value-system. This acquiescence is not primarily defensive, not a struggle for political or economic or other form of equalization. It expresses itself in affirming the integral individuality of one's person, of taking on freely the obligations that go with it; of insisting not on becoming *like* anybody else, but on having one's singularity recognized and acknowledged as possessing a title equal with any other's to live and grow.

Now this sort of self-acquiescence is the personal premise—whatever be the pattern of grouping—for the group belongingness, the group identification for which one name is cultural pluralism. Alain Locke made this choice as a grown man, just as Walter White made this choice as a boy in Atlanta, when he experienced the violence of a mob of whites.

For Locke's disposition had been first monistic or universalist. Pluralism and particularism imposed their reality upon him by the exigent harshnesses of experience. It is these which convinced him of the actuality of difference, which brought him to recognize that difference is no mere appearance, but *the* valid, vital force in human communication and in human creation.

The transvaluation had never seemed to me to be quite complete. As you can see from his "psychograph," Locke chooses to speak of it as a rationalization. He would have preferred reality to be basically a One and not a Many, and human relations to be expressive of this Oneness. His preference interposed an active reservation to the actuality of the plural. It long kept him from completely committing himself. Philosophically, it led him at last to the concept of ideological peace.

I have spoken of Locke's essay, "Values and Imperatives." There is another he wrote and, apart from his doctor's thesis, I don't know of any more philosophical studies by him. The second he called, "Pluralism and Ideological Peace." As I read the essay, which he contributed to a collection entitled, *Freedom and Experience*, edited by Sidney Hook and Milton Konvitz, "ideological peace" again involves an association of the different which requires our making a distinction between unity and union. The import of Unity is liquidation of difference and diversity, either by way of an identification of the different, or by way of a subordination and subjection of the different to the point where it makes no difference. *Per contra*, the import of Union is the teamplay of the different. Union resides in the uncoërced, the voluntary commitment of the different to one another in free coöperation; an ideological peace, as Locke had expounded it in this essay, is a conception denoting fundamentally this free intercommunication of diversities—denoting the cultivation of those diversities for the purpose of free and fruitful intercommunication between equals.

To the American Negro it presents the idea of an authentic Negro cultural community sensitive not only to the positive values of all the present, but aware also of the immemorial African past and rendering it presently a living past. Of course, this past is not in the memory of any living American Negro. He must needs create that memory, by means of exploration and study, as Locke did and just as every white must; indeed, as the record shows, identification with African cultures and arts can be more passionate and more complete among white men than among Negroes. To many, perhaps to most, the import of the term "Afro-American" is unwelcome. For Negroes tend to reject such an identification because they perceive themselves to be penalized on account of this same African difference. So long as a person thinks of himself as being penalized as African, so long as he is not self-acquiescent, just so long will he resist identification with those presumed sources or conditions of his imposed inequality. The hyphen represents a bondage, not a resource or power. Let him absorb and digest the condition, turning it from a limiting handicap into a releasing endowment, and he frees himself.

This, it seems to me, is what Locke did. And hence, in his discussion of the New Negro, Locke was able to talk about the Negro problem as a creation of non-Negroes which they imposed on the Negroes. As anybody knows who has lived through the abominations of Senator Eastland's Mississippi in the past few months, Locke's analysis is correct.

The Negro, Locke held, is not a problem. The Negro is a fact, an American fact, but not merely because he has lived and labored in America since Colonial times. He is American in virtue of his commitment, in common with non-Negro Americans, to the essential American Idea, the idea that human beings, all different from each other, are equal to each other in their inalienable rights to life, liberty, and the pursuit of happiness, and owe each other participation in the joint endeavor "to secure these rights" on which the institution of government rests in free societies. All "these rights" may be comprehended as the right to be different without penalty, without privilege, and with each of the different maturing its own excellence, the excellence expressive of its individual or associative singularity in willing coöperation with all. Believing this, Alain Locke gave expression to his own commitment to the Negro fact by undertaking to disclose to Americans, especially to Negro Americans, the Negro, not the problem. He made himself the philosophical midwife to a generation of younger Negro poets, writers, artists.

However it is a very delicate and difficult undertaking to separate any existence from the problems of this existence. This challenge confronts all communities everywhere, not alone the American Negro community. And it is far harder to effect this separation where a community is penalized for merely existing. Hence, one cannot be sure that Locke succeeded. But one can be sure that, without the affirmation of Negro as Negro in terms of what cultural and spiritual production Negro as Negro can achieve, without the manifestation of inner strength based on self-knowledge, developing without tutelage from anybody, the Negro cannot begin to accept himself as a fact instead of a problem to himself. One can be sure that where such a process eventuates, the

Negro problem transvalues into a white problem, both south and north. And one may observe that the problem "gets liquidated" wherever communities of diverse identity do thus accept themselves. An orchestration of their diversities follows, a teamplay of their differences. The concept "race" wouldn't apply to these differences since any species whose members can breed together may be said to belong to the same race. First and last the differences are the specific differentiations of personal and group existence that make cultures, that make systems of ideas, creeds and codes about which human beings fight. "Race" is one such fighting word. Color constitutes no problem when it is not appraised in racist terms. Transactions between peoples of different colors in the same culture and different cultures in the same color, and different colors and cultures have gone on freely enough throughout recorded time. Alain Locke urged that they can go on here at home. He held that they would have to be postulated on what he called ideological peace. In his essay on "Values and Imperatives" he urged that this peace might be attained by the conceptions and the methods of science. There is, he declared in that essay of 1935, "an objective universe," whose unity is broken up into a pluriverse by human behavior.

I think that in the twelve years between the first essay in 1935 and the second in 1947, he decided that primarily there is a pluriverse, and that ideological peace is the endeavor to establish a universe, not as a unity, but a union. His pluralism reshaped into a primary, a fundamental pluralism—a value pluralism, a metaphysical pluralism, and the reshaping may have involved something like a religious conversion. As he believed, it is a way of changing your own attitude toward yourself, and your own attitude toward the different. First one needs to recognize the integrity and autonomy of difference; then perhaps one can also peaceably do business with it. In point of fact, Locke had already done so in "The New Negro," although his philosophic realization seems to have come later.

There are two current words which signify ideas that have a present bearing on this notion of free coöperation of the different, or ideological peace. One of these words, signifying an American policy, is "containment." And what does "containment" mean? It means forcefully holding back the different. Why did we have to have a national policy of containment? Because of Communist aggression against what is not Communist. Perforce it is to be held back, and unless the resistance were equally strong or stronger it could not be held back. Outer containment depends on inner moral and material strength. Whether or not we achieve the political end, it continues morally and culturally on the agenda for the American people, and of our Negro fellow-Americans *vis-à-vis* certain categories of non-Negroes.

The second word is a word that came into vogue after "containment" had become a policy. The word is "co-existence." There are different ways of co-existence. There is the co-existence of cold toleration signalized as balance of power; here powers stand over against each other at alert and ready to shoot— the way the South Koreans had to stand against the North Koreans, the Israelis stand against the Arabs, and the entire West stands against the Soviet and its satellites.

In another phase, co-existence signifies passive toleration. Each existent says to the other: You're there and I've got to recognize you are there, but I don't like you and I won't have anything to do with you. You may be a brother, but you're no neighbor and no friend.

In still another phase, co-existence signifies what we now usually mean by toleration—that is, not an inimical endurance or suffering of the different, but a recognition that the different can live and let you live and that you can live and let the different live. Co-existence means live and let live.

The mature phase of co-existence comes whenever existents pass from this sort of *laissez-faire* into a free, a voluntary coöperative relationship where each, in living on, also helps, and is helped by, the others in living. This is the co-existence that cultural pluralism signifies. It is the consummation of the system of ideas and the philosophic faith that Alain Locke became a notable spokesman for.

His speaking consists of the two philosophic essays I have referred to. I think it might be a project for the memorial group to bring these essays together, perhaps with his doctoral dissertation, and publish them as a posthumous volume.

I don't know of anything else in strict philosophical discussion that Alain Locke has produced. But those two, brief and compact as they are, signalize not only the high place of his own philosophy of life, but a view of human relations that is bound to become more and more the hope and desire of the great majority of the peoples of the world.

Thank you.

12 | This Is My Faith

Introduction

1. In *the Judaeo-Christian religions*, stripped of their divergent ethnic, doctrinal, and structural factors, what religious values, *as you use the term religion*, do you think should be emphasized in contemporary thought and practice?

2. In the light of *the worldview that modern science is unfolding*, what grounds have you for religious convictions about cosmic reality? Do you think that it cares for man's well-being? If you think that it does, how do you reconcile your convictions with such evidence as Nature's apparent indifference to the highest interests of man and its occasional destructive treatment of him?

3. Are the human values expressing *the genius of the democratic movement and of personal moral character* intrinsic elements of your religious faith? If not, what relative place do you accord them in religion? If so, are they the sole grounds of your religious faith? And, if so, why?

4. Do you assume that *the supreme values available to moral man, of whatsoever source*, are aspects of *one* spiritual reality? If so, how do you relate in your faith the survival values of the Judaeo-Christian religions (question one), the dynamic values inherent in the activity of the cosmos (question two), and the creative values emerging in man's struggle to build a society of free men (question three)? If not, how do you relate these various value-structures in your conception of spiritual reality?

5. Does *the concept "God"* serve an essential purpose in your rationale of religion? If so, what is the particular content of your inference when you use this concept? If not, what is your source for knowledge and guidance with respect to the highest type of human life?

In reflecting upon the questions to which this paper is a proffer of answers, I undergo a feeling of irony that spans their entire theme. The very subject—"the foundations of human purpose and values"—starts it. "Foundations" suggests permanent grounds for stable superstructures. It implies that the grounds are somehow inalterably the same, however the superstructures differ from one another. The particle "the" accents the suggestion. It implies for the reader that, whatever be their nature, there are, there can be, no other foundations. They are *the* foundations, infallibly such-and-such, always and everywhere the same one eternal and universal order behind and beneath the world's multitudes of peoples; its manifold configurations of beliefs, preferences, and performances supporting, holding up their "purposes" and "values" as Atlas supports the world. By implication, foundations are the unchanging ground of change, the safe and certain matrix of the changes and chances of the human struggle for existence which the words "purpose," "value," signalize. By implication, their changeless substance is more valuable and meaningful than the processes of ongoing change, of hazards and challenges which are the stuff of history and biography. Unitary origin counts for more than diversifying consequences in the diverse struggles of the diversities of *Homo sapiens* for their diverse survivals.

"Purposes" and "values" signify these diversities; they name formations of the matters, the media, the satisfactions and frustrations which men's struggles come to and go from. In any individual life, they signify the shape of its ongoing propulsions; they are terms of passage with significances that only the future can validate, and the future enters everybody's experience as a diversification of familiar sameness into surprising difference; an individual's future is the news in his life. To live on, and by living on, presently to suffuse and alter the ongoing past with events and experiences which neither repeat it nor inevitably follow from it, is to create this news, which differs from individual to individual, and compounds into the indefeasible uniqueness wherein each distinguishes himself from every other. The self-creation is also what we usually call "struggle for self-preservation," "struggle for survival"; it is what the diversifications of being born, growing up, and growing old diversely count up to, at the stoppage whose other name is death.

These consummations, at once unique and manifold, are, however, what the religious and philosophical systems of our "great tradition" refuse to accept. They call them mere appearances, deny that they truly evince the human condition, and argue variously and inconsistently with one another to prove that the experience of life and death is an experience of unreality, and the reality is an external and universal foundation that repeats itself in man as inalterable soul which cannot die. Their aspiration continues to be one of replacing the human condition with a set of foregone conclusions: that though it is to live on, yet it is not to change; to purpose, yet to have its purpose already realized; to desire, yet already to be possessed of what is desired; to value, yet not to need to struggle for the existence of values. They argue that we cannot want what we do not already have, nor become what we yet are not, and that the contrary witness of experience is *maya*, illusion.

A common symbol of this reality behind and beneath the apparent human condition is "Heaven." With it go a whole congeries of terms, bespoken by such expressions as "supernatural," "immortal soul," "spirit," "angel," "God," "Devil," all receiving meanings as concrete and singular as the cultures they figure in, and all in themselves constituting, for the meaners of those meanings, "the substance of things hoped-for, and the evidence of things not seen." In the discourse of their users, they serve as value-words: that is, words whose meanings are inward to the words themselves. Searchers for something else than the words, for forces and forms that the words signify, regularly come back to individual or collective attitudes, actions, hopes, fears, facilitations, frustrations, or their configuration into churches and other institutions. They never attain to any open sharable experience of "objective" substances and evidences, such as commonsense and the sciences rely upon. The words and other symbols are terms of faith, not knowledge; themselves all the objects, the substances, and the evidences that faiths are faiths in. They bespeak the ever-insecure and troubled human person, struggling to be safe and untroubled yet alive at last. But they do not purport the endlessly varying circumambience of nonhuman things and events amid and with which the sons of Adam wrestle, as Jacob, with the Lord.

That nonhuman is usually called "nature," and its stuffs and sequences can be discerned, explored, defined, and known. The entities postulated by the value-words are usually called "supernatural," and can only be believed-in. "Nature" is equated to "existence," the "supernatural" is equated to "value." Thus "value" would be one of the differentiae, perhaps the most critical differentia, which signalizes the humanity of the human being—the difference wherewith human existence distinguishes itself from other existences, the natural singularity of *genus humanum*.

It would follow that a humanism which, whether as a philosophy or as a religion, concerns itself with that in men which establishes them as human, would first and last value the entire diversity of valuations. To deny or condemn any one of them for what it is, and not for its consequential relations with different valuations, would be to cultivate a defective and less-than-human humanism. If, as Protagoras is said to have held, man is the measure of all things, of things that are, that they are, of things that are not, that they are not, then the "values" wherewith the sorts and conditions of mankind measure themselves, their fellow-men, and their nonhuman circumambience are the constituting energies of their being as men, each different from the others and none more privileged to be itself than any other.

The maxim of Protagoras would be falsified if any by original nature had a better title to struggle for its existence than any other, or freely to endeavor to excel in the consequential arts of measurement than any other. Those are the arts whose tests in experience are the diversifications of unfree and narrowly conscious human existence into ever freer, ever more dynamically comprehensive awareness of self and the world. The Biblical term for this propulsive self-orchestration of diversifying consciousness is "the life more abundant." Albert Schweitzer, proclaiming "reverence for life," embodies this intention of "man the measure" alike in his personal history and in his reasoned faith.

I now turn to the five questions. What answers I can produce will be congruent, at least to the extent that my intention and desire can make them so, with the beliefs I have just set down.

I

If "religion" signifies what I perceive it to signify, then to strip "the Judaeo-Christian religions" or any other, of "their divergent ethnic, doctrinal, and structural factors" would be to denature them. It would be to treat them as a chemist treats a compound when he deprives it of its qualities *as* compound, and reduces it to simpler residues. His analysis destroys; it neither discloses nor discovers the compound's *identifying* characteristics, for that compound is a whole whose parts are so related to one another that each has come to be qualified by all. Its concrete identity is a consequence of those relations. When they are severed, it perishes. What ensues is something quite other, in quality and action as different from the compound as hydrogen and oxygen are different from the water into which they are usually combined. The religions of mankind are complex historical growths. They do not put on and take off their divergent ethnic, doctrinal, and structural factors as a man his clothes. Rather, the factors figure for the religions of the world as a living man's lungs and

liver and other organs figure for the man. Together with the residual creeds and codes, rites and rotes, they compose the diverse
"organic" configurations that are the distinguishing *whats* of the
global multitude of religions, of which the Judaeo-Christian ones
are a few.

History records sequences of such configurations, all altering
as they struggle to live and grow, some carrying the tradition
which their alterations compose through millennia, others failing
and falling apart in the course of a few centuries, a few generations, a few years.

That which makes the difference between long life or short,
survival or extinction, is not *what* the configurations are, but *how*
their faithful believe in them. Any person, any image, any idea,
any pattern of behavior, any social institution, and any configuration of them becomes an object of religious faith when a believer
so believes in its bearing on his existence and destiny that he bets
his life on it; and it is reliably *his* religion only so long as he bets
his life. Then, be it a theism, an atheism, or any other *ism*, he
trusts it as the insurance of his victory in his struggle to live, even
when he dies. Thereby he endows it with supreme value, and he
will talk and work and fight for it against the other faiths of
different believers. To him the latter are then infidels, heretics,
rebels, traitors, and foes of eternal life who must be extirpated if
possible, and silenced, or contained and restricted, if not.

Now a certain phase of contemporary thought and practice
recognizes that in such a war of all religions against all, each believer intends for himself what he would deprive the others of.
Each insists that the end on which all agree can be attained by his
means and only by his means. All want life more abundant, each
according to his kind, and each insists that the way to this life is
his way and no other. Since the Protestant Reformation men have
come to recognize that any and all religions, however set up, are
diverse communities of collective means for the consummation of
the life more abundant as a distributive end. They have come to
recognize that religions are made for men, not men for religions.
So they have come, in their thought and practice, to pass from
mutual aggression and warfare to the grudging balance of power
which is the first form of toleration, from that to the more gener-

ous rule of *live and let live* which is toleration's second form. And they are now at points in passage to the third form, whose rule is *live and help live*.

In this passage, the emphasis properly falls:

First: On perceiving each religion as a cultural whole of faith and works.

Second: On endeavoring to understand sympathetically the individuality of this whole: to accept and respect its existence; not to aim to conform it to one's own religion on pretensions to exclusive God-given superiority and truth.

Third: On cultivating such free and friendly communication between different religions as would consummate in a union of each with all that would guarantee to each alike its freedom to live and to grow in safety and equality. As I have shown in *Secularism Is the Will of God*,[1] such a union of all faiths—*in pluribus unum*—would compose a global communion that could grant no favors to any nor commit itself to one more than to any other; it would be a whole, with qualities and functions different from those of its member parts, and *Secularism* is the word which signifies these qualities and functions.

II

I do not consider that modern science is unfolding one and only one worldview, or that it is committed to any. Science, insofar as it *is* science, is an ongoing method of inquiry, changing and improving as it goes on. The reliability of *what* a science discloses accrues to it not from *what* is disclosed but from *how* it is disclosed; from the trust in the method, not the character of the object. Just now some men of science are monists and determinists who work in the faith that all differences can be liquidated in an identity such as "energy" and all changes conformed to unchanging laws of change. Other men of science are atomistic pluralists and indeterminists who work in the faith that "reality" is a manifold of fluidities and processes that compound as they con-

[1] (New York: Twayne Publishers Inc., 1955).

tinue, and that cosmic evolution and human history are better accounted for when new beginnings are added to ongoing sequences, and chance and probability complement invariant laws. And there are other scientific worldviews less postulated on the disclosures of scientific method. All may, as such, become "religious convictions," and do; or they may be used, as by Compton, Jeans, Eddington, Whittaker, and others, to supplement or to confirm the more conventional "religious convictions" which assert that some immanent or transcendent total consciousness similar to human reason or will or feeling is an all-ruling providence which benevolently shapes all ends, whoever rough-hews them and however.

But there are also those who believe in a Devil as well as a God, a hell as well as a heaven, to say nothing of a purgatory, and to these, Malevolence can be as real and as rational as Benevolence. For some, like the Manicheans, all existence is a practically equal struggle between the two, in which the final victory of Benevolence is inscrutably remote. On the other hand, for persons whose faith is firm that God is omnipotent Benevolence, their faith creates the well-known "problem of evil." So far as any man's personal history is concerned—he is born, he grows up, he grows old, he dies. From birth to death his existence consists of a struggle to go on existing. The struggle enacts itself as a gathering, making, storing, using, consuming whatever supports it; as dispersing, destroying, shutting out, and cutting off whatever is felt to be seeking to quell it. During some of its phases life is heightened and advanced; during others, life is contracted and retreats. Often, the forward phases occur at the cost of the freedom and existence of other men, always at the cost of soil and sea, of animals, plants, microorganisms. During phases of recession, these others reverse the roles; earthquakes, storms, eruptions, floods, plagues, and poisons destroy the works and flesh, and check and subdue the spirit of man. If "indifference" [2] means that "Nature"

[2] See, for example, Chapter XII, on "Altruism" in Sir Charles Sherrington's *Man on His Nature*, (Cambridge: Cambridge University Press, 1951), where he recounts from "almost countless many" the life-cycles of Redia, the parasite of sheep-rot and of plasmodium, the parasite of malaria, with their ravening, torturing blind pilgrimages from host to host, animal or human. "Life's prize," Sherrington comments, "is given to the aggressive and inferior life,

evinces no hierachy of values, plays no favorites, has no chosen breed, human or nonhuman, then nature is "indifferent." That whatever is born dies, whatever begins ends, and that nothing on earth is seen as unbegun and as going to no end, is an observation tempered also by another observation: that the sequences between beginning and end often do compose themselves into orders of excellence, better and worse, and that because this happens, philosophers and theologians and historians do choose one such order to use as the measure of praise and blame for all: one need only mention St. Augustine, or Oswald Spengler, or Houston Stewart Chamberlain, or Henry Adams, or Arnold Toynbee. In the context of their worldviews, "indifference" would mean deterioration or rejection. But in other contexts it also could mean the formation and growth of excellences without any care for their duration: they could come to perfection and perish. There are people who bet their lives that God is both good and omnipotent whatever happens; their faith is, "Though he slay me yet will I trust in him." If they die trusting, have their values been invalidated? Can existence for them be said to have been indifferent or malevolent?

III

I presume that "genius of the democratic movement and of personal moral character," refer to the ideals of human nature and human relations set down in such public credos as the American Declaration of Independence and the global Universal Declaration of Human Rights, and to ongoing struggles to incarnate the ideals in the works and ways of the world's peoples. I think I can say that they underlie the creed and code I bet my life on. I believe with a firm faith:

(1) that people are irreducibly different from one another and that this difference is an inalienable right, to be exercised by all alike, without fear or favor, safely and freely,

(2) that the right extends to every form of the human enter-

---

destructive of other lives at the expense of suffering in them, and sad as it may seem to us, suffering in proportion as they are lives high in life's scale."

prise—religious, cultural, educational, political, economic, scientific, and so on,

(3) that people best secure these rights to themselves and to one another by joining together in corresponding societies, little and great, which serve them as collective means to their distributive ends.

Yet, if I were a Brahmin, I might concede and reverence the right to be different without penalty to cattle and vermin, but would penalize certain categories of other human beings for their difference. If I were a Buddhist, I might concede the right to all living things and contract my own existence as man to the mystic's minimum, ultimately to the nullification of my humanity. If I were a fellow of some one of the "Judaeo-Christian" communions, I might concede the parity of those groups whose rights I was not strong enough to disregard to overrule. Then I might "tolerate" their differences, but condemn or deprecate and scheme to translate them into agreement with mine, whether in their hearts they agreed or no. If I were a certain species of Humanist, I might take either attitude toward non-Humanists.

As a Secularist, however, I recognize the equal right of all the world's different faiths to be what they are as they are, so long as they do not cancel this right for themselves by refusing it to others. Although it cannot be said that the world was more made for man than for any other living thing, the world's peoples, when they unite their different strengths and skills and wisdoms, can and do remake it for themselves. As their local cooperative unions associate into a global one, the remaking becomes global, *in pluribus unum.*

IV

There are assumptions in Question IV as put whose disclosure and analysis my present task has no room for. Just now I can only say: Mankind being what it is, the "moral man" of one society may be, and is, the "immoral" or "unmoral" man of another, and that the "supreme values" of one may be, and are, condemned as the reverse, by another—that, in some, different groupings manifest different ways of life, different standards of living, different personal embodiments of both.[3] The values are many and the moralities are many, each varying from the others, each having the others for near or distant neighbors. The neighborly relationship may be tantamount to a warfare of moral ideals. It may consist of hot war of all with all. It may pass from that to cold war, thence to "coexistence," and at last to the free trade in things, thoughts, and beliefs wherein neighbors become "good neighbors." The relationship between "good neighbors" may be described as a pooling of means in a shared endeavor to help each other attain their individual unsharable ends. It is the collective or public table which satisfies the singular and private hungers. Insofar as any oneness comes here into play, it is a consequence, not an initiation. The initiation is in the indefeasible plural hungers; the oneness in the consequently pooled means of their satisfaction; it follows from and resides in the union of the many, and its reality has for its sufficient reason the reality of the many.

Whether I should regard such a reality as "spiritual" would depend on what is meant by this many-valued word. Assume that it is being used as priests and other churchly people use it. Then it signifies an Otherworld of one or more substances, each an individuality invisible, imponderable, impenetrable, indestructible, always and everywhere the same. The conventional names of such substances are God, Devil, angels, demons, souls, and the like. Collectively they compose "the Supernatural." By definition utterly different from the natural Thisworld of matter where we struggle for our existence, this supernatural Otherworld of spirits providentially infiltrates, permeates, and surrounds Thisworld, influences our motives and conduct, shaping our fortunes for both worlds. But the action is not one-way, down from the heights of spirit to the abysms of matter. Enfleshed man can affect discarnate spirit, prevent it from hurting, persuade it to helping. Such working on the supernatural becomes the specialized vocation known as priestcraft, that expertise in doctrines and disciplines which is required for the profession of middleman between Supernatural persons and natural human beings. The means and tools of the

[3] See the article "Morals," *Encyclopedia of the Social Sciences* (New York: The Macmillan Company, 1948), Vol. 10, p. 643.

profession are nature's lands and buildings and other properties, vessels, vestments, meats, breads, wines, and other sacrifices, chants, songs, preachments, all ordered into the rites and rotes, the modes of worship and prayer, which diversely signalize the diverse cults of the supernatural. By their means, the specialist in the manifestation of the supernatural practices his art on behalf of the "material" and "spiritual" needs and wants of his cure of souls.

"Spiritual" here has a meaning organically related to the economy of a religious corporation, competing, like other corporations, for more abundant material support, prestige, property, and power. Different meanings go with different configurations of experience and organization. All might be regarded as changes whose matrix is a man's primal awareness of his own breathing. His *in*-spiration and *ex*-piration are movements and pressures felt, heard, but not seen. The Old Testament word for spirit is *ruah*; Greek *pneuma*, and it variously signifies invisible wind, the hot blow and the cold. Within man, *ruah* is the angry, the sad, the fearful blow of his breath, or the zealous, the hopeful, the triumphant one. Outside man, *ruah* signifies the invisible élan which pours itself out upon, rushes or falls upon, passes over upon men —who thereupon prophesy—and which is here, there, everywhere, nowhere, beyond beholding or imaging. The *what* of *ruah* is a passage too mobile for perception to catch; only the *how* of its passing is felt and the consequence of its passage known.

In the New Testament—essentially the Pauline documents— *pneuma* figures as that indiscernible inbreathing (ultimately the Holy Ghost) which sets Christian apart from non-Christian— God's grace, the free gift he gives, or pours out into, the true believer, who thereby becomes one "reborn into the Kingdom." Finally spirit as invisible mobility ends up in Spirit as invisible immobility. It is consolidated into that unitary, impenetrable, imperishable entity for which the commonest name is Soul.

Now, although a soul's mortal span is crowned by an immortal destiny, its theological identity is unaltered and unalterable in both. Although it thinks and wills and feels, it does not change; only its place and status change. Yet its mortal breath of life consists of a sequence of Thisworldly transactions, conscious and unconscious, with Thisworld's material circumambience, whereby it both learns and forgets. The transactions diversify and combine as refinements of perception, as discriminations ever more delicate and precise among thoughts and things and events, as their orchestration into a confluent pattern wherein each is appreciated via its relations with all. On occasion, this ongoing process enters a phase when it is suffused and lit up by a glow of positive feeling which signalizes a kind of closure; the individual has wholly committed himself to the vision he beholds, and his seeing has become his conspectus of understanding and guidance for his life, his light upon existence and destiny. This event is the individual's *auto da fé*. That which he now affirms has become the object of his faith on which he bets his life—the substance of things hoped for, the evidence of things not seen, and so the substance of spirituality. It is this not in virtue of *what* it intends, but in virtue of the *how* of its intending, and of its uses. So, we speak of the spirit of a people, a culture, or a cultus, the scientific spirit, the spirit of the laws. These are not primal stuffs but ongoing attitudes and behaviors, leaving residues in the works and institutions of men. Students of the past may infer them from the residues; but as the life of living men they are addressed to the breeding of the unborn future. The sacerdotal Otherworld of souls and spirits appears, in the light of such spirituality, a materialism addressed to accumulating property, prestige, power, and people. Organic relations between that supernaturalism and this spirituality are as rare and accidental as such relations with any of the separate and distinct Thisworlds, which together compose the nature that science studies and the arts remake in order to meet the exigencies of human nature.

V

From what I have already set down, it would follow that the symbol "God" has multiple roles in my "rationale of religion," and that these roles are attributes of the multitudinous concretions—some seventeen hundred different major divinities alone have been counted—of image, attitude, idea, force, function, and mystic experience all given the name "God." Conceptually,

"God" is used to designate one chosen from the multitude to the exclusion of all the others—indeed, in enmity and warfare with all the others—and thereby in recognition that they are, and are rivals of the preferred divinity. That one is the "true God" of his faithful devotee because the latter is betting his life on his God's grace to save him from the compulsions of fate, and on his God's providence to save him from the accidents of fortune. The believer's religion is his theory and practice of bringing grace and providence to his aid.

The symbol "God" may also be used to denote all the gods of all the faiths taken together, not pantheistically, but as a free, federal union acknowledging, respecting, and conserving their individualities but orchestrating their functions in such wise that the faithful of any may feel assurance of help in need from the faithful of every other. Or, like certain mystics, a believer may feel that the Divine Many, with all their diversities of conception, image, creed, code, rote, and rite, are but protean disclosures of an ineffable One utterly opaque to conception and imagining, and endlessly reshaping itself into concepts and images, all symbols, none disclosures. The experience on which this view draws is beyond verification. Being unique and ineffable with each mystic, it is incommunicable and beyond proof and disproof. But unless disproved, its authenticity may not be doubted. The faiths of which it is the matrix are another matter: their deliverances and practices can be set beside each other, analyzed, and compared, and their singularities, overlappings, and inconsistencies displayed.

On the other hand, to their incommunicable and hence indiscernible mystic matrices, Leibnitz's rule of "the identity of indiscernibles" may be applied. This would compenetrate the ineffable Many into an ineffable One, the source of the Many. So the devout Hindu mystic, Ramakrishna, committed himself wholly to the divinities of his own land, to Allah of the Moslems, to the Christian pantheon, and "realized God" in all alike. He went from the Many to the One.

But the many creeds and codes and cults which are assumed to issue by interpretation of the One cannot be rendered thus identical. Their diversifications continue indefeasible. Oneness for them all must be, as for Ramakrishna, eventual free achievement, not necessary antecedent condition. The Godhead of their discourse is the diversity of Gods whose faithful tend to war against each other for the greater glory of their chosen One, whose reign on earth hence is not, but is ever to come. Bringing the state of war among religions to a covenant of peace between them requires at once the obsolescence of the conception "God" as a primal unity of which the world's multiple pantheons are shadows and reflections, and its replacement by the idea of Godhead as a free union whose diverse members are acknowledged for the realities they are in the cultural economies of their faithful. In that union is their peace. Religious pluralism is the *sine qua non* of interreligious peace, even as cultural and national pluralism underlies intercultural and international peace. For peace can be had only in a union of the different wherein all covenant equal freedom and security to each.

I do not, however, find in the record any unquestionable ground for connecting this belief, or any other with either "the highest type of human being" or the "lowest." Different families and ages of mankind are still far from a consensus regarding "highest" and "lowest" and are always likely to be. For these appraisals are differentials of the singularity of the struggle to live and to grow of each individual, of each society of individuals, and of each society of societies. The course of the struggle may exalt now one type, now another, as the Christian Gospels suggest.

For myself, I would rather dispense with such invidious terms of appraisal, which denote alterable relationships to altering interests, not unalienable qualities and rights. I prefer to place my faith in the parity of the different, the equality of the unlike, and their collective guarantee of this equality to one another: this is the thing not seen that I hope for, and its substance and evidence I gather from the record of the peoples of the world. I am well aware of how selective and *ad hoc* is my gathering.

13 Secularism As the Common Religion of a Free Society

Not so long ago, the clergy of all cults and denominations tended to write or speak the word *Secularism* in a manner eloquent of discomfort or anxiety or anger or hatred. There was nothing in dictionary definitions of the word to account for the emotional disturbance. Webster, for instance, identifies the secular as "belonging to the State as distinguished from the Church" and again "non-ecclesiatical, not religious in character nor devoted to religious ends or uses." The secular is thus the concern of the laity as against the clergy, and *Secularism* is the lay frame of mind. Since the clerical vocation depends for its social role and status on its relationships with the laity, the passions stirred by the word *secularism* would seem to have another object than the laity as laity. Clerics anxious or angry or hateful toward *Secularism* must needs conceive what it signifies not only as a concern of the souls in their care, but also as an infidel way of life and thought tending to atrophy the clerical function in society and ultimately to dispense altogether with the priestly vocation and its many and diverse occupational organizations! Because the latter, severally and jointly, identify themselves with "religion," they charge that *Secularism* is necessarily inimical to "religion," although as a rule "religion" means to them their own particular creed and code and no other.[1] If they include others in the category, they are apt to qualify them as false religions and to identify them by such names as "superstition," "magic," "voodoo," "idolatry."

For them, by and large, Secularism intends not the freedom *of* religion which it claims, but freedom *from* religion; that is, they say, "freedom from God," and how can anybody be free from God as they imagine God?[2] In sum, Secularism is displayed as religion's all-time enemy, ever to be contained and conquered. The more established and orthodox the clerical interest, the more ardent the aggression against Secularism; the less orthodox, the less aggressive, and the more sceptical about the motives of the aggressor. Thus in 1948 the Bishops of the National Catholic Welfare Council declared "Secularism . . . is the most deadly menace to our Christian and American ways of living," [3] while the late Methodist Bishop Bromley Oxnam, writing in the *Churchman* in March, 1952, warned: "Protestants must be alert lest in a blind march on 'Secularism,' they become allied with forces that would destroy public education, deny the right of private judgment and shackle the free mind." Some five years later, Bishop Stephen F. Bayne, of the Protestant Episcopal Church, sometime Chaplain at Columbia University, told a dinner meeting of the Division of College Work of the National Council of Churches that Secularism is "a dirty word"—"the enemy—the front." But now—shall one say, *mirabile dictu?*—comes Bishop John A. T. Robinson of the Church of England and a former Cambridge don,

[1] See R. S. Spann (ed.), *Christian Faith and Secularism;* Denis de Rougement, *The Christian Opportunity:* . . . "secularism is the confiscation of the spiritual riches of Christianity . . . It is atheism brought into the real world, organized, lived and daily practiced, but progressively stripped of its controversial elements."

[2] Cf. Charles E. Rice, *The Supreme Court and Public Prayer* for a repetition of recent theologizing of this point by Jesuit writers as context of a discussion of the Court's decisions.

[3] Cf. N.Y. *Times,* November 20, 1948.

with a book that he entitles *Honest to God*, arguing that the traditional God of sacerdotalism had best "be redefined in secular
rather than religious terms." And the head of England's religious
establishment follows with a commentary entitled *Image Old and
New* written in somewhat the spirit of Sir Roger de Coverley
with a view, I guess, to preserving the union of divergences which
in doctrine and discipline the Church of England seems to have
become, but sympathetic neverthelsss with Dr. Robinson's rein-
terpretation of his Church's faith.[4]

The issues raised follow, obviously, from the event that people use the words Secularism and Religion with a variety of meanings. The belief that the two must be foes turns on the meanings
which the user chooses.

Now we create meanings by taking attitudes toward any
content of our experience to which we can give a name or which
recurs unnameable. In various degrees we accept or reject the
perceptions, images, concepts amid the flux of which we struggle
to live and labor and be ourselves. We believe in them or disbe-
lieve in them. We have faith in them or regard them as untrust-
worthy. Some we strive to get ever closer to and ever more and
more of; others we flee from as we can, striving to cut them off
and shut them out from the world of our experience. Always we
dispute which to cling to, which to repel. We do this whether we
take them for real or apparent, fact or fantasy, thing or symbol.
We do this whether we regard each as unique, as manifold individualities recurring, or as a self-identical One, always and everywhere the same. Each—no matter how we soon or late account
for it—is in and by itself a presence that we have become aware
of and experienced as a help or hindrance in the struggle to keep
on struggling that custom calls self-preservation. Philosophies,
theologies, sciences of man and sciences of nature distinguish the
differences between these formations of our experience by many
names and conflicting appraisals. But however they identify and
appraise them, none is so much concerned with what it presently
presents as for what it portends for the non-existent future. He

---

[4] An interesting scholium is the late California Bishop James Pike's suggestion
that the dogma of the Trinity is expendable, and that there would be practical gains from dispensing with it. (N.Y. *Times*, Aug. 31, 1964).

takes it for what it is now in itself only incidentally to the unexperienced consequences that are to follow it. Here and now it is but a sign, a symbol, a prophecy, a forecast, a promise or a threat of what is to come. In the struggle for self-preservation, the meaning of any presence is not itself similarly present; its meaning is its future consequences—"the shape of things to come," the *after*life with its *where* and *how*. All religions, worldly as well as otherworldly, manifest this ineluctable concentration on man's future and labor to invest that with a local habitation and a name. For all that preserving oneself first and last consists of, is living on, indefinitely having a future, if also after one is dead.

Both this-worldly and other-worldly religions are formations of men's strivings to define and make certain an ambiguous and indeterminate future, ever not quite definable or sure. This-worldly ones, with their sciences of nature and man, the other-worldly ones, with their other-worldly disciplines, are alike professions of faith as St. Paul defines faith: the substance of things hoped for, the evidence of things not seen. Each cannot but be a configuration of beliefs about the future, chosen from a manifold of such. Their divergence and antagonism—if any—is about *what* faith takes for its substance, *what* it accepts as evidence, and *how* to regard the substance and the evidence. Each other-worldly religion holds that its own stays one and the same, always and everywhere. Each sincerely this-worldly religion holds all to be a diverse manifold, altering with the changes and chances of experience. The articles of faith of the other-worldly are eternal, universal and infallibly true and their method, therefore, mostly dogmatic and dialectical. Their logic is the logic of a closed system. Per contra, the articles of faith of bona fide worldly religions are working hypotheses ever undergoing validation by future consequences and open to alteration in the light of the consequences. Their logic is the tentative logic of exploration and discovery, open to a future of chances and changes. Since all living is a bet on the future, both logics are such. But the other-worldly religions make their bets as if the future were a sure thing, while the this-worldly ones bet believing that the future is not a foregone conclusion.

The paramount divergence between this-worldly and other-

worldly faiths, then, is procedural. The difference obtains also
with respect to religions which, in their antagonism to the traditionally other-worldly, declare themselves worldly, but are in substance other-worldly. For the authentic worldly get to the substance of their faith by way of discovery and to its evidence by
consequential verification; the other-worldly get to both substance and evidence by way of revelation, which is a disclosure of
that which cannot be discovered or known otherwise and is intended by the revealer to save mankind from its earthly plight by
defining the world and ordaining a way of life which shall assure
them all always and everywhere the safe and certain future they
all keep struggling for. The traditional words for that which revelation reveals are "God," "the supernatural." But the salvational
powers which these words signify also are attributed to other energies signified by other words—energies eternal and universal,
revealing themselves as infallibly as their implied rivals and as sure
a thing to bet the future on, however consequentially valid be the
alternatives which compete with them, whatever be the future
that actually ensues. The alternatives, being mortal error, are to
be denounced, suppressed, subverted or destroyed.

The most familiar contemporary instance of such an atheistic
other-worldliness or Godless supernaturalism is the revelation of
Dialectical Materialism by Karl Marx according to Lenin.[5] The
articles of this faith turn out to be as essentially irreconcilable
with the discoveries and methods of the natural sciences in Soviet
Russia, as the articles of the other-worldly faiths of the freer
world. It needs no forcing of an analogy to regard Soviet Russia
as a Church State with an infallible State Religion, to which domestic organization and foreign policy are conformed and recon-
formed until, at the inevitable long last, when the true believers
have won their inevitable victory over all rivals, they shall on the
principle, *extra ecclesiam nulla salus*, impose upon all mankind the
creed and code which alone can make secure for them everlast-
ingly the Marxist future that their existence is an unwitting struggle for. True believers in the articles of the faith form the Com-

[5] Cf. V. I. Lenin, *Materialism and Empirical Criticism;* David Jorarsky, *Soviet Marxism and Natural Science*, 1917–1932.

munist Party; its rank and file are "the believing church"; its hierarchies of functionaries from the Central Committee downward and outward, form "the teaching Church." Its theology is called ideology; its theologians, theoreticians. Appointed guardians of the faith, its defenders against the errors and subversions of deviation within and heresy without, they must see to it that the sciences of nature and of man, in conflict with Dialectical Materialism, shall be conformed. If they cannot be conformed, they must be suppressed or denied—as has been done with non-Lysenko genetics, with relativity and with quantum mechanics. True, in so far as physics and chemistry are factors in the Soviet political and military economy, their practitioners are free to disregard Communist orthodoxy. But when it comes to public expression, their deliverances must be fitted to the articles of faith of the Establishment—or else. If the Party's Central Committee is its Curia, then its various Academies of Sciences and Arts and their Institutes are its Sacred Congregation of the Holy Office, charged with combatting heresy and protecting the true faith. As is usually the case in the history of ideas, divergences and innovations keep arising and the censors and inquisitors lead a busy life.[6]

However fixed and infallible any creed and code whatsoever may be said to be, whatever be their substance and evidence, the generations of mankind keep diversifying them into ever more numerous doctrines and disciplines which their aficionados combat with every available means. Each, the persistent and the divergent alike, consists of a profession of faith concerning the determinations of its Supreme Power regarding the future of man. Each insists that alone the articles of its faith are infallibly the true intent of its ineffable revelation; that its rivals are errors or deceptions whose *terminus ad quem* is not life ever living on, but eternal death. Each insists that human beings, in order to save their Selves alive must—be the cost in suffering and sorrow what it may—put aside their errors and illusions and commit themselves to the one true faith. In consequence, the history of religions is

---

[6] See Siegfried Muller-Marens, "Soviet Philosophy in Crisis," *Cross Currents*, Winter, 1964; Lewis Feuer, "Meeting the Philosophers," *Survey*, April, 1964.

the record of a diversifying struggle for dominance among religious societies, and of religious societies against non-religious societies. It is a chapter of the Hobbesian war of all against all.

In what is now being called the Judeo-Christian culture, the Protestant Reformation brought this war to a new turn. By asserting "private judgment" as an unalienable right, and attributing priesthood to all believers, it took their freedom of conscience for granted, and repudiated sacerdotal claims to sovereignty over the meaning of revelation and to divine authority for penalizing divergences in creed and code. Claiming that all men are equal before God, it denied the claims of the clergy to privilege. In effect, the wars of religions which the Reformation roused initiated changes in the relations between church and state and church and church: and between both and the individual layman, now entitled freely and safely to make his own decisions concerning the will of God regarding the ways and works of mankind. These changes have tended away from religious wars to inter-religious peace, as similar changes in political relations have tended to sustained efforts toward international peace.

One expression of the tendency is the six propositions about freedom of religion, agreed to by spokesmen for the world's miscellany of creeds and codes, in the Universal Declaration of Human Rights. They are developed as consequences of the article of faith with which the Declaration begins: "Everyone is born *free and equal* in dignity and rights." One of them (Article 2) denies that *any religion* has a right to impose limitations on anyone's title to this equal liberty. Another (Article 6) specifically asserts this title in issues of *marriage and divorce*. A third (Article 18) reaffirms it respecting "freedom of thought, *conscience and religion,* freedom *to change their religion and alone or together to teach, preach, worship and observe their religions.*" The fourth (Article 26) declares that education, one of man's unalienable rights, must seek "the full development of the human personality and the strengthening of the fundamental rights and freedoms by promoting tolerance and friendship among all nations, racial or *religious* groups." The fifth (Article 29) forbids limitations on any of the declared freedoms and confines restrictive legislation to "*due recognition and respect* for the rights and freedoms of others and of meeting the just requirements of morality, public order and the general welfare in a democratic society." The sixth (Article 30), forbids any and every perversion of the meaning of the Universal Declaration for the purpose of justifying conduct of "any state, group or person" which aims "at the destruction of any of the rights and freedoms set forth herein."

Now this universal declaration of human rights makes no reference to God, the Devil, Godless Materialism, Devilish Supernaturalism nor any other specification of the providence which shapes our ends, rough-hew them how we may. It is a profession of faith, not a description of fact, stating the substance of what mankind hope for in all human relations, not alone the religious. Its propositions are the evidence regarding the wished-for interpersonal and intergroup relations which they do not see. Like the "Agreement of the People" formulated by the Levellers of England in 1647, like the next century's American Declaration of Independence, both of which do use the word "God," and like the American Bill of Rights, which does not, the Universal Declaration professes a faith not alone Christian, Judaist, Moslem, Mormon, Shinto, Vedantist, Buddhist, Taoist, Confucian, Humanist, Communist, atheist, or any other congregation of true believers, but a faith to which they in their diversities subscribe together. It is the profession of a faith by mankind for mankind in the only sense in which "mankind" can signify concrete reality. Thus the Universal Declaration would assure to each and every religion— be its supreme being what you will—equal right with all others to struggle for its survival and growth without penalty and without privilege.

It must be apparent thus that the *What* and the *How* of the Universal Declaration are not identical with those of the miscellany of faiths it would bring to equality in rights. Indeed, its *what* and *how* are one and the same. Its object of faith is a procedure, a method, a transaction involving its terms and principles in a sequential configuration of relationships. Admitting each of the multiplying miscellany as it presents itself with its distinguishing creed and code, the Declaration would as such so relate it to its neighbors that all may continue together equally free and secure. As doctrine and discipline, the Universal Declaration neither competes against nor replaces any other; it supplements them jointly and severally. Common to all and identical with none, it provides the terms of the covenant they may complete with one another whereby all undertake to safeguard the liberty and security of each against the aggression of any. These terms postulate the right of private judgment, the priesthood of all believers and the separation of church and state, with their consequences in the hesitant but ongoing democratization of religious establishments, the historic shift of ultimate religious authority from the professional religionist to the laity, the attrition of the traditional privilege of clergy and the multiplication of denominations and churches with democratic organizations and diversifying creeds and codes.

On the record, the conspicuous field of this course of religious events is the United States. During the stretch of years from Franklin and Paine and Jefferson and Madison to Holmes and Brandeis and Black and Warren, Americans have come more and more to believe that the faith animating this sequence, which is being both lauded and damned as Secularism, can so equalize the status of religious societies before the law; that none may lawfully seek special privilege, none may lawfully be laid under special penalties, that all may freely and safely profess what they choose to profess and live as their faith directs them to live. Americans have come to believe that these articles of faith can and do achieve for interpersonal and intergroup competition an ordered and just liberty which manifests itself in the interfaith and intercultural movements and in the cultivation of the "dialogue" that are characteristically American. The stand of American prelates of the Roman church regarding *aggiornamento*, the right of private judgment, and regarding anti-Semitism at the Ecumenical Council, Vatican II, is another and notable expression of the American belief. The entire record suggests that the American people severally and jointly supplement their manifold, diverse and diversifying religious beliefs with another one, different from them all, which they hold in common—the belief which commits them separately and together to assuring to one another the equal liberty and equal safety of their particular faiths.

Call what you will the salvational power which has revealed

itself in and through the articles of these faiths—God, Nature, Spirit, Matter, and so on. In so far as it saves by those means and no others, it cannot and will not be the saving power invoked by the others. The power which saves all alike must intend the parity of the different as different; it must intend their relations to one another as equals. Among the other-wordly, such an intention cannot be anything but this-worldly, that is, secular. As the *what* of a faith different from, yet common to, all the growing miscellany of other faiths in a free society, it is Secularism. Among Americans it goes with the word "God." Regardless of the multitude of diverse and diversifying conceptions employed to give it some one definite and fixed meaning, Americans insist on stamping or printing it on their money and on public documents, pronouncing it on public occasions and teaching it as the name of overruling power in their public schools. The diversity and conflict of meanings seems no matter; the reality the word should intend is not the common thing; the word's the common thing.

If, however, the articles of their common faith are taken for the revelation of an ever-hidden reality which the word "God" signifies, and not simply for the discoveries of ongoing experience, then the divine reality which they reveal but cannot present must be incommensurably different in nature and power from the Gods of the miscellany of creeds which shut each other out and cut each other off. Believing in it as commensurable but adds one more to the miscellany of conflicting identifications. It adds still another confirmation of Santayana's statement, in *Reason in Art*, that the word God is "a floating literary symbol, with a value which, if we define it scientifically, becomes algebraic. As no experienced object corresponds to it, it is without fixed indicative force and admits any sense which its context in any mind may happen to give it."

But on the record, secular as well as non-secular mystics do use the word to signify an experienced object—an object, however, ineffable; an X, subject of all predicates, identifiable by none. The very up-to-date theologies seem to take their stand on this ineffability. They remind one of an observation by the cartesian priest Nicolas Malebranche: *Quand je vous parle de Dieu, si vous me comprenez, c'est que je me trompe.* I have in mind especially Paul Tillich's revelation of his "God above Gods" in his *Courage to Be*, his *Deus Absconditus*, the hidden God who is, he asserts, not the god of theism or pantheism or deism or hinduism or other such *isms*, who is not a "supergod" yet at once is and becomes, forever "beyond" every institution and establishment, every image and symbol, every segregation of theist from atheist, holy from secular. We must, nevertheless, "out of inner necessity name this ineffable, unknown, and unknowable Beyond, "God"; also "God of those who reject religion." If will may be attributed to "God" so meant, Secularism, not as the creed of one more church but as the faith common to the ever-multiplying diversity of churches other-worldly and this-worldly, may, but need not, be designated as "the will of God."

14 What I Have Learned, Betting My Life

When I ask myself what, over my too many years, I have learned, I find that I'm not asking what it is that I have come to know beyond any doubt, but what it is that I have come to believe in enough to be willing to bet my life on it, aware that no bet can be a bet on a sure thing. I find that I owe the articles of my faith far more to the give and take of direct experience with places and persons, with their thoughts and their things, than to the discourses of the schools or the writings of the scholars, whether ancient or modern; and I find that I have a certain pleasure in examining the latter's writings for confirmation of my own credo —particularly if the confirmation defeats its author's intentions.

This may impress today's many—who cultivate "analysis," "semantics," or "philosophy of science" in order to grow the certainties which their Beat Generation no longer harvests from their elders' "perennial philosophy"—as another fall into the meaninglessness which they allot to meanings they do not accept. My

165

meaning may figure for them as but another absurdity vainly interposed to delay their infallible deflation of the philosophies of the great tradition. Perhaps they imagine rightly, for I am, I believe, by disposition and habit, a philosopher, and I have been by training and lifelong occupation a professor of philosophy. The latter does not necessarily follow, not to say follow from, the former. I have been lucky.

I am not sure when I recognized that one learns as one lives, and that the consummation of learning is more like undergoing a conversion than reaching a conclusion; the challenge, the anxiety, the travail are in unlearning the old far more than in learning the new. I became convinced of this early in my personal history, and it has stayed a gradient for my thinking about learning and teaching ever since. That which I found myself unlearning was a configuration of professions and practices embodying beliefs about Man, his world, his role, and his destiny in it, which I had become committed to, unknowing. I had grown up somehow living by them, yet feeling ever more troubled and afraid. What I learned and became converted to is the philosophic faith I have been confessing, reasoning about, and trying to give effect to in words and works these fifty years. It identifies me as a libertarian who had been a determinist, a temporalist who had been an eternalist, an individualist and nominalist who had been a universalist, a pluralist who had been a monist, without being alienated from what he had been. The sum of it—a Spinozist who became a pragmatist.

What I now believe about Man and how he got to be what he is in his becoming, about the ends and means which give form to his struggle to keep on struggling—that some call "existence" and others "survival"—is confluent with this philosophy; it orchestrates, I trust, the articles of this faith. With them, I am able to acknowledge the singularity of each event of experience as it passes, yet to find it as meaningful as the Christian drama of salvation renders the banal flatness of the communion wafer meaningful for the true believer. Yes, any philosophy lived as well as spoken can effect a like transvaluation. Only, the perennial ones must needs reduce events to unrealities, and then, in order to render them meaningful, each must needs practice its own mode of transubstantiation on them, while the analytic and semantic ones go on debunking every such transubstantiation into nonsense and futility.

As I see our life now, it is of the singularity of Man's manhood to practice transubstantiation. Everybody's doing it, everywhere. Everybody's creating his peculiar fetish, which shall secure him against his peculiar insecurity. Among the most highly relied on is "reason." The transubstantiation of the facts of reason into the diverse fetishes of rationalism and supernaturalism and scientism are among the most approved and emulated of human ways. The practice endows the passing experience, whatever it starts and ends as, however in itself banal, with saving power on which the true believer bets to win for himself the future he wants. Although to me it discloses the illusions that men's hopes generate, I may not grudge them those illusions, precious and real in that they are felt to guarantee the hopes. Willy-nilly, men live on by betting their lives and thereby investing what they bet on with the role of a magic engine of victory in their struggles to keep on struggling. This I have learned by unlearning.

Learning it has been an ongoing initiation, a rite of passage, from the dogma that the real is the One—One God, One Universe, One Humanity, One World, One Law of Nature, One Rule of Life for All Mankind—that the foreordained consummation of the last would be, "under God," universal brotherhood and universal peace. These onenesses comprised, in essence, the articles of faith of the orthodox Jewish household of my childhood and youth, which cleaved unto them regardless of their daily repudiations by events.

Repudiations were diverse. A pervasive one was anti-Semitism: My father, a Russian subject, serving as under rabbi in the small Silesian town where I was born, was *ausgewiesen* by Bismarck's Prussian government as an alien Jew. He found his way to Boston, where he brought me up in the faith of the fathers from my fifth year. In Boston, on the streets and in the schoolyards, the Christian kids taught me what they had learned the Jew should receive in payment for the salvation from eternal death which the death of their crucified Savior brought them. I could endure, and on occasion even overcome, because I knew that I belonged to God's Chosen People and that my pangs and pains were linked in some salubrious way to the divine election.

But the Christians ganged up not only on the Christ-killers; they ganged up on one another, however Christian—as Protestants, as Catholics, as Yankees, as Micks, as Wops, as Polacks, as Dutchies (there didn't happen to be any niggers; these appeared later)—all, even as I, innocent carriers of the ways and views of their elders into the streets and the schools. At school, ever and anon, there came ceremonial occasions when the entire miscellany of pupils had to stand up and intone, "I pledge allegiance to the flag of the United States and to the Republic for which it stands; one nation indivisible, with liberty and justice for all." I don't recall whether the pledge was pledged "under God"—that phrase was added after my time as a student, under Eisenhower, I believe. I do recall how more and more puzzled I became each year I grew older.

The natural sciences which were a part of my schooling— physics, chemistry, biology of a sort—only deepened my puzzlement. For they seemed to subordinate unlike and incommensurable happenings to identical law; they seemed to digest the changes and chances we experience into a sequence of necessary connection which dissipated freedom in fantasy and novelty in illusion. The sciences, assimilating all differentiation into a system of eternal and universal Identity, always and everywhere One and the Same, yet refusing to identify this One as God in any form, I imagine, both confirmed and confuted the ancestral faith.

However, one day I chanced upon a German rendering of Spinoza's *Theologico-Political Tractate.* It set me free. I began to read English versions of his works and English commentaries on them. It was in the year of my graduation from high school that I became enamored of the man and convinced of his philosophy. His image, his thought, and his story became the point of no return in the ongoing alienation from my father and the ancestral religion. I identified with Spinoza. The reader may, if he wishes, write "unlearning" for "alienation from" and "have been converted to" for "identified with."

At college I was made aware of monisms other than Spinoza's, each purporting to be the only true one and to expose any alternatives as mistaken in fact and false in reason. They made up a diversity of competitors to be recognized as the unique revelation of the One which is, beyond every doubt, always and everywhere alone the Same. What I was reading and learning about religion and science disclosed a like rivalry. Both told of ongoing struggles for the establishment and continuation of beliefs—each at one time taken for true by some minds and false by others—all sooner or later displaced by different ones which had been rendered more acceptable to the same minds or others of their kind. The "body of knowledge" I saw was an ever-changing body in which truths of the past become errors of the present, and truths of the present are struggling not to be reduced to errors of the future. How, then, could anything "real" be always and everywhere the same—even Spinoza's substance, his *deus sive natura?*

What I had painfully learned is that the condition of fallible people was the condition of their infallible truths, no less! It made no sense. And how could one keep up the struggle to keep on struggling unless one could make sense of it? William James, who "gave up logic" and developed reasonableness, showed me how sense might be made of it. All I have learned since the time I first came under his influence has its vital root in the man and his teaching.

The empiricism I learned from James is "radical." It takes not only the events of experience as they come, each with its own singular presence, it also acknowledges the reality of the multiple ways the singulars join together and move apart, no less identifiable than the presences they relate. To perceive any is at the same time to perceive its helping or hindering the struggle to keep on struggling which from birth to death compounds into the person that one goes on becoming. An event's role in the struggle makes its value for the struggler as he strains to assimilate it into all else that he has already appraised as true, false, good, bad, right, wrong, beautiful, ugly, rational, absurd, reality, appearance, meaningful, meaningless. He labors at an ongoing identification of the diverse; and everywhere in the world, every variety of mankind's endeavor is a striving to transvalue the diversities they encounter into some One they choose to take for the one Real, and for the harmonizing ground and goal of the embattled manynesses —the One which somehow guarantees their everlasting safety and well-being.

That no inquiry has yet disclosed such a One, that each quest adds one more figure to those already demonstrated and advocates one more way of reaching it, seems not to abate the ardor of the quest. Let the seekers be Albert Einstein hot for his Unified Field; let them be his epigones striving to overcome the ongoing multiplication and diversification of their briefly ultimate particles by means of an overruling "symmetry"; let them be Julian Huxley projecting an Evolutionary Humanism, or Teilhard de Chardin spanning creation between the Alpha and Omega of his transcendentalist evolutionism; let them be Norbert Wiener and his epigones, with their cybernetic grounding of the computerization of human relations and of the scientific, religious, political, and cultural economies they shape up. Each envisions some singular unity responsive to his particular business and desires. The unity continues to be a hidden unity, ever a *deus absconditus*, ever believed in, never encountered—an article of faith, not a fact of experience.

Men know from birth how much of life is a war of the faiths, each becoming different as it struggles to master or destroy the different ones that beset it and to attain incarnation as fact by itself alone. Each unity is at once the end and the means of the warfare. The earliest fact, and the latest, is differences increasing and multiplying, with *Homo sap* struggling to lasso and harness their circumambience for the varying uses of his struggle to keep on struggling. And when a harness is believed so to serve, the user changes its status, giving value precedence over existence; he translates his tool into an idol and worships it exclusively for the goods and services he hopes it will provide. So *Homo sap's* inveterate fetishism has until this day transvalued his pecking orders and his gods; so the priesthoods of the present age transvalue the arts and sciences. The fetishism sprouts from what William James has called "a certain blindness in human beings."

He started me toward a cure of this blindness, and it began where I lived. My unseeing had come with a dumb anxiety over my Jewish identity. Non-Jews were troubling my days and nights because, through no fault of my own, I happened to be different from them. My difference diminished me, shackled me, deprived me of my liberty and subjected me to injustice. I must needs rid myself of it and make myself the same as my apparent betters. I must needs change from Jew to—what?

None of the people I was encountering were, in each other's esteem, themselves undiminished by some differences; and all, even the weakest and most humble, seemed to be penalizing others as they could for not being the same as themselves. Following Spinoza, I had come to believe that difference, seen clearly and distinctly, made no real difference, that in substance all the families of mankind are one. What I had learned about the faith that shaped the Republic at first reenforced this belief. Did not the Declaration of Independence tell the world that "all men are created equal, that they are endowed by their Creator with certain unalienable rights," among them "life, liberty, and the pursuit of happiness"? That men institute governments in order to insure the unalienable against alienation? That the just powers of government rest upon the consent of the governed who institute it? So what could "equal" mean, save what it used always to mean—"the same"?

Yet in the business of living, "equal" signified not sameness perceived or achieved but scorning and fleeing some particular difference—by an individual, scorning and fleeing whatever keeps him, with all the self-diversification that growth is a word for, *this* one and no other; by a group, scorning and fleeing a style of living, thinking, working, and fighting together—a culture, a self-altering tradition of faith and works which joins the group's members to one another. As it obtains, the group's association is a process of union, not a state of unity. Some unions are shotgun marriages, enforced by preponderant power, as among racist and other totalitarian formations; others get their shape from the free teaming up of their members, and grow more cohesive and powerful as their uncoerced participation prolongs—which is the case among the freer societies. I have learned to qualify the varieties of the latter as orchestrations, and to signalize education as the vital center of their survival and growth, which indeed it continues to be in every society.

During my youth "Americanization" became, here at home, the word for manifold ways of dissipating differences, all directed to self-alienation by the different. One favored way was unquestioning conformity to requirements of those who claimed to be the nation's élite and used their power to enforce their claims. Another, not a little resisted by the claimants, was to emulate them, more widely signalized as "keeping up with the Joneses" or "bringing up Father." Still another was willy-nilly melting the Joneses together with oneself into an undefinable new superidentity in Israel Zangwill's "melting-pot." The true American of the future was to be this unique homogenized new *Homo sap.*

As I pondered such often violent divergences, it came home to me that the different signers of the Declaration could never have meant their "laws of nature and of nature's God" to intend "the same" and write "equal." For thus, the divine intention eliminates no differences; it only sanctions one kind of difference, taking privileges and laying penalties on other kinds. So, what is not the same cannot be "equal"; what is different is required, *as different,* to stay unequal. No person, no faith, no occupation, no way of life, no culture might sustain its identity and be equal in those human rights declared to be self-evidently unalienable, and against whose alienation Americans declared their revolution. Was not this Declaration discounted as "glittering generalities," "self-evident lies," or held to be valid only for "superior races"? Does it not continue to be so appraised, everywhere in the world?

The revolutionary meaning of "equal," however, repudiates such appraisals. This means by "equal" equal *as different;* it affirms the parity of the different; it recognizes that their equality does not abolish their diverse natures but preserves and liberates them, jointly and severally to live on and to grow, to succeed or to fail, by their own power, on their own merits, at their own risk. "Equal," I came to believe, intends the right to be different as *the* unalienable right—so long, so cruelly, and so diversely subjected to alienation—of which all other rights declared to be unalienable develop as diversifications. I learned that, at least for *Homo sap,* "to be" and "to be different" are synonyms for the

reality of his struggle to keep struggling; that my Jewish difference could be no less real, worthy and honorable than any other I
might be fleeing to; that unlearning it might more greatly diminish me than living and orchestrating it.

And if this were true of my Jewish difference, how not of
my friend Alain Locke's Negro difference, which had presented
this poet, scholar, man of letters, and philosopher with a challenge
of identity far more poignant and critical than mine? We talked
much about answers to it the year we both were at Oxford. And
if my Jewish and his Negro difference are ours of right and not
by sufferance, then, in the nature of things, so are all such differences. It was, I recall, during my talks with Locke that I first used
the phrases that have become clichés—"right to be different,"
"cultural pluralism," and "pluralistic society."

My experience elsewhere than in my field nourished the perceptions which the clichés named, and the reasonings they crys-
tallized. I found that my pragmatist pluralism shaped my reflections about persons and peoples, nations, religions, arts, sciences
—their economies, and their rivalry and cooperation with one
another. Their *de facto* diversities, not their *de jure* onenesses,
stayed in the foreground of my sentiment and the reasonings it
prompted. I came to judge the onenesses as either imaginative aspirations compensating for lived actuality, or projects to reshape
actuality closer to the heart's desire. *E pluribus unum* became for
me the directive agreed upon by a configuration of individuals
and companies whose communions joined them into communities
of culture as diverse, and as diversely associated, as themselves.
The generations of them somehow pledge themselves, as they
come, to maintain their union of differences in such wise that all
together undertake to assure to each separately equal liberty and
equal safety.

Such undertakings would, if successful, be the actuality of
peace. As things are, peace is a multitude of struggles short of
war. Like war, it suggests a search for a moral equivalent. I have
come to believe that the Republic must, among other things, be
also such an undertaking, which its citizens covenant to advance
and protect from ongoing aggressions within and without, old

and new—aggressions which keep on testing, as Abraham Lincoln observed at Gettysburg, whether a nation so conceived and so dedicated can long endure.

To date, the nation *has* endured. So far, from the Civil War on, the American people have, against no little resistance, tugged and pushed, bullied and bawled their country into less imperfect actualizations of the declared rights of the different to equal liberty and equal safety. Someone's always doing it with regard to the economy at home and the circumambience abroad.

Since the turn of the century, disputes among Americans have mostly concerned the doubted means, not the declared ends, of the world wars, hot and cold, and of the local wars between and after. Few, if any, have challenged Woodrow Wilson's great design "to make the world safe for democracy"; or Franklin Roosevelt's projection during World War II for "survival" of his "Four Freedoms"; or John Kennedy's reformulation of both as struggling "to make the world safe for diversity"; or no-less-utopian Lyndon Johnson's recent "We have learned to despise the witch hunt, the unprincipled harassment of a man's integrity and his right to be different." Few, if any, have challenged the manifold specifications of the right to be different that compose the Universal Declaration of Human Rights, whose professors purport to represent almost all the peoples of the world. Not a little in consequence of the American experience, even the Roman hierarchy, through Pope John XXIII's Ecumenical Council, has given reluctant recognition to men's right to be different and to their joining together to assure to one another equal liberty and equal safety in differing.

That Mankind's professed goals may be, and largely are, pretensions with which they mask practices is so all-pervading a commonplace that it need only be mentioned. The record, however, discloses that professions can and do project new goals with new ways and means to them; it has persuaded me that to date, at least, the ever-revolutionary American credo and the American people's experience and reformulations of it have prompted societies everywhere on the globe to turn to new goals and to seek new ways of which the beginning without end is the right of the different to equal liberty and equal safety.

Does the record as I read it bring me confidence that *Homo sap's* struggling will achieve its goal? What odds do the statesman, churchman, scientist, or bookmaker give on peoples' diverse struggles thus to live on? How do I bet, in view of the once unimaginable odds these struggles have created since the turn of the century? In view of the new knowledge and the new know-how incarnate in the engines that harness atomic power with atom smashers, atom bombs, automation, computers, rockets, and new chemicals? In view of the anxieties, the tears, the fears, the preoccupation with death, including the death of their gods, which the rationalizing Cassandras of the gospel of absurdity celebrate and demonstrate?

Having learned that reason serves best as neither a power nor an energy but as a prophecy before, or an accessory after, the event, that the event is the decision after decision which compounds into the individuality of each one's struggle to keep on struggling, decisions to which reason serves as a viable aid or a formal hindrance—I bet on the struggler over event. I do not see that, first and last, any human life requires a sanction from any other existence, human or nonhuman, natural, supernatural, or unnatural. Nor do I find this a cause for tears and not for laughter; existentialist tearfulness seems to me as comic as perennial philosophy's cheerfulness. The circumambience, however its components be imagined, discovered, or constructed, comprises the conditions of each one's struggling on; if any become an authority that a struggler relies on, or a master he believes, obeys, and fights for, it is by the struggler's consent, because he has so taken it.

I do not see that extinction by dying can in any way render meaningless the living of life as it is lived. The living makes its own meaning, *is* the meaning, is all the meaning there can be. For each person it consists of this and no other singularity of faith and works struggling on, maintaining its integrity. Long or short, lives end with death; they become the nothing that they were before birth; their meaning perishes with them.

Epigones who afterward study, evaluate, reprobate, or worship the image they make up from a dead person's less perishable residue endow it with meanings or meaninglessnesses which but utter their own business and desires. To itself, no life lacks meaning, even if, like some professors and poets, it cultivates its own meaning by charging everybody else's life with lacking any. For all lives, their going on is goal enough.

Every so often I recall Job, challenging omnipotence, declaring, "I have no hope, I know that he will slay me; nevertheless will I maintain my ways before him. Mine integrity hold I fast and will not let go; my heart shall not reproach me so long as I live." On occasion, I recall how Pericles told his Athenians, in that unforgettable funeral oration, that the secret of happiness is freedom and the secret of freedom a brave heart. On other occasions I remember de Tocqueville—"The man who asks of freedom anything other than freedom, is born to be a slave."

I do not believe that in the nature of things there are many such askers. I believe that those whom others judge to be such are individuals who, still struggling against alienation of their unalienable right to be who they are and to become what they want to be, get so absorbed in securing the means to their freedom that they lose awareness that it is also the unalienable, all-deciding beginning and end which chooses and changes the means. Like Arthur Miller's salesman who died, they become aware again, if only to die.

Having learned and unlearned as I have, I find myself disposed, when I encounter such an awareness, absurdly to seek consolation from the feelings it arouses in the ever-resurrected cliché of a laughing Roman: *Homo sum; nihil humanum a me alienum puto.* Its absurd peer, in my own vernacular, would be: *There, but for the grace of Lady Luck, go I.* If I have become a secularist and a humanist, it is on these terms.

15 Dialogue with Dr. Horace M. Kallen, by Ira Eisenstein

I.E.: Dr. Kallen, the occasion for this visit is your recent retirement from active work at the New School. How long did you teach there?

H.K.: I gave my first class with the opening of the New School in the spring of 1919.

I.E.: That was 50 years?

H.K.: Yes, almost 51. The New School was radically new—an innovation in higher education—trying to develop what Kurt Lewin called, in his own field later, action-research, to bring together academic scholarship with the practical problems of human relations, which, with the First World War, were likely to develop as crisis after crisis. The idea of the School took form as a consensus of journalists, college professors and citizens with a concern for the future of the United States as a free society, and for peace and freedom under law among the peoples of the world.

The journalists were chiefly on the *New Republic*. The editor, Herbert Croly, had written a book *The Promise of American Life* which deeply impressed the Morgan banker, Willard Straight and his wife Dorothy. They felt Croly's views should have wider circulation, and enabled the launching of the *New Republic*. Croly recruited a notable board of editors—outstanding among them Alvin Johnson, whom he took from the Economics Department at Columbia, Walter Lippman, who had been secretary to an upstate socialist mayor, as well as professional literary journalists like Frances Hackett. He included many college professors among his contributors, myself one of them. Chief among the academic founders of the New School were the historians Charles Beard and James Harvey Robinson. And among the public spirited citizens were such notables as Emily James Putnam, Mrs. Thomas Lamont, Henry Bruere and others. The plan was to have open enrollment—no entrance examinations, no credits, no degrees. Men and women of any age or equipment could come to inquire into the problems of contemporary society under the leadership of members of the faculty who would also be available for consultation and guidance for students who planned to teach, write or both. I myself began with a small seminar on "The International Mind; its nature and conditions" in the spring of 1919.

I.E.: Did they bring you from Wisconsin?

H.K.: No, I had left Wisconsin more than a year before, over an issue of academic freedom, which was created by a faculty vote to condemn Wisconsin's great Senator, Bob LaFollette, as "giving aid and comfort to the enemy." LaFollette was a pacifist on principle, and this happened to fit in with the pro-German sympathies of his largely German-derived constituency, and of many members of the Faculty who had studied in Germany and remembered their time there with pleasure and a kind of loyalty. After we were sucked into the war, LaFollette stuck to his guns. The shoe being on the other foot, the Faculty turned on him. The vote directed the chairmen of departments to circulate the condemnation among the members for signature. I refused to sign. I had studied in Germany a bit; I am German-born; but I hadn't gained the feeling of certain of my colleagues for the academic *Deutsch-*

tum or any other kind. This had nothing to do with my father's having been expelled from Germany as an alien and a Jew; it had to do with the difference I felt between German and English and French academic personages and academic ways.

I.E.: I have an idea that you developed something of the fervent patriotism of many people who came to this country—a patriotism which very often outshone that of the natives.

H.K.: I wouldn't put it that way. I would say I grew into a commitment to the American Idea. As I recall my schooling in Boston, where I grew up, its cultural base was Jewish. Indeed, I have an image of a maternal aunt standing over me as a three year old, and dropping a coin on the book when I read a letter correctly. This was in Europe—I was luckily brought here at five. But the main provider of my Hebraic base was my father. In a sense, it's a taproot. Things come back to me of this time of my life more vividly than many things I learned later. They become continually more important. Aging is a form of entropy and the coordinations and orchestrations of which growing older consists break down after a time. The parts of the past move centrifugally from one another. The energies dissipate. Degrees and tempos of entropy differ from person to person. Think of Bertrand Russell at 97.

I.E.: You developed a very fervent love of American principles.

H.K.: There was an evolution, yes. But I wouldn't say it was due to the conditions of life in Boston's Jewish ghetto. The group and cultural conflicts in Boston were not different, in terms of human relations, from such as you find in any community. I sketched the situation in an article for the *Saturday Review* which Norman Cousins reprinted in a collection titled "What I Have Learned." My beginning is in the discipline and rigid order of an Orthodox Jewish household, the head of which was a *k'lai kodesh*, supplemented by a somewhat looser control in *heder* and a still looser discipline, but a discipline in the elementary and grammar schools I attended. Boston's public schools in the early 90s were good by comparison, of course. At the Eliot Grammar School there were two men teachers—civil war veterans, and the principal was a colonel. One of the teachers—as I talk to you I see him: his name was Granville Sylvester Webster. He had muttonchop whiskers, the kind you see on youth nowadays. He had the Yankee twang, the Yankee sense of humor. He used to read the class stories, and he knew, of course, who my father was, and it used to amuse him to stop me in the corridors, before the bell rang—the men were acting a kind of police—keeping order—and they talked religion and theology to me. Webster was an agnostic. The other, Benjamin Hinds—big, squat, very much younger than Webster, very handsome, with a very black moustache—used to stand alongside, and I could see both were amused. I used to resent being stopped, but the conversations left their mark. Besides the classes bored me. Every so often Webster or Hinds would drop some idea of freedom. Hinds taught American history. The picture made in the textbook was conventionally eulogistic, non-critical, prejudiced. It contrasted sharply with the actual experience on the street, in the crowds; and with the idea emphasized, the ideas of the Declaration of Independence, the public profession we would make on occasion, "one flag, one country," etc. Those professions are articles of faith, not descriptions of behavior. They are articles of faith which are supposed to guide and control behavior, but are disregarded, just as all law which guides and controls behavior is constantly disregarded in different ways. This raised the question, what is the real faith, how far does any person live up to the professed one?

I.E.: How did you relate this to your Jewish upbringing? Did you get any of these ideas from your Jewish teachings?

H.K.: No, my Jewish teaching was a discipline. It was ritualistic; it was *Shulhan Arukh*.

I.E.: Nobody tried to combine the two?

H.K.: Oh no. In those days nobody would except perhaps Unitarians. Not only Jews; no "Christian" Christian would. An atheist was taboo in all circles, including the Harvard circles, when I finally got there, although Santayana, for example, was an atheist.

I.E.: A Catholic atheist.

H.K.: He was an atheist who rejected Catholicism without alienating the Catholic ways of thought, just as I reject Judaism without alienating the Hebrew Jewish ways of thought. You see, the issues shaped up to a kind of inner, intellectual confrontation.

I.E.: Did you work this out yourself; I mean this relation of your Jewishness to your Americanism?

H.K.: I lived it out. The thought came as a realization of what I had lived . . .

I.E.: When you say how you lived, what are you referring to? Your Zionism?

H.K.: Oh no. I didn't get in to Zionism . . . You see the internal devaluation of Jewish heritage was continuous and progressive. My father was a strict man; I didn't like him; and my mother tended to stand between him and me, between him and the rest of us. I was the oldest of a family of 8—6 girls, my brother, the youngest.

I.E.: The oldest always get the toughest role.

H.K.: Not necessarily always, if he is the firstborn and nobody follows.

I.E.: If you're that kind of oldest you're in a good spot.

H.K.: It was a poor household and the rules were such that the *orehim* (guests) were always more important than the members of the family. At the Sabbath meal father would have in guest visitors; then, it was FHB—family hold back.

I.E.: Well, these were values which, while they weren't verbal, must have impressed you somehow.

H.K.: Of course they impressed me; they stay with me now.

I.E.: But what part of Judaism did you reject?

H.K.: Say rather, discard—devalue: the theology; the coercive ritualism, all the impositions of *halakhah*.[1]

[1] The laws and regulations of Jewish observance contained in the Talmud.

I.E.: When you absorbed these values, they became, in a sense, self-justifying.

H.K.: You mean when I "returned," when I became first tolerant, then understanding and sympathetic to the Judaistic rites and rotes? Of course, it took time and it took a good deal of reconciliation and identification with the American Idea. The Jewish Idea, as it had come to me, was the antithesis of the American Idea; and for that matter the American Idea was, in terms of Declaration of Independence and the Preamble to the Constitution and the Bill of Rights, also the antithesis of the Christian Idea. For that matter, the Universal Declaration of Human Rights is such an antithesis.

I.E.: Then in a way the American Idea brought you back to Judaism?

H.K.: Not only "in a way," Ira. This story I've told a great many times.

I.E.: I know you have, I'm just trying to get a resume of it now.

H.K.: Well, you see it wasn't really the American Idea that brought me "back," or perhaps better, forward. It was the disclosure by a teacher who might be called a Tory Yankee with Puritan heritage, with an ancestry traced, if not to the Mayflower then somewhere close. From Barrett Wendell I came to understand the role of the Old Testament in the organization of the Congregational churches as against the Episcopal or ecclesiastical, as liberation. It justified the formation of a free religious society and the movement from congregationalism to the notions of equal liberty of all religious societies.

I.E.: And not just individual liberty.

H.K.: Individual liberty within any society is first rebellion, then rule. In terms of the Universal Declaration of Human Rights it is rule for all mankind.

I.E.: Did you develop any ideas of collective rights?

H.K.: Those were automatically involved, because you can't think of our Declaration of Independence or of the Universal

Declaration except as intending a society of equally free peoples. The plural *peoples* is my contribution. Cultural pluralism signifies acknowledging the diversity and equality of peoples and their cultures.

I.E.: About when were you developing these ideas?

H.K.: I was a sophomore at Harvard when I had this course with Barrett Wendell. I had these teachers, Barrett Wendell, William James and George Santayana, and tangentially Hugo Munsterberg, a converted Jew who remained sympathetic to Jewish connections, and Josiah Royce who had the totalistic, Hegelian approach, but who Americanized it in quite a different way from the traditional American Hegelian.

I.E.: His stress on the community, you mean?

H.K.: Yes. That was of his latest conception. To his notion of the Beloved Community, his concept of loyalty to loyalty and others of that kind, he came to as positions philosophers do come to. I hold them to have been functions of his personal history, of problems domestic and other.

I.E.: Many questions are asked, and I'm sure you have had them asked of you: granted that there is this distinction between Jew and Judaist, granted that the Judaist element is not for you, not attractive, you're left with this Jewish identification. Why should one continue it, if it is possible to eliminate it, particularly if maintaining it produces penalties which one could perhaps avoid by becoming something else, identifying yourself with some other group? Particularly if you're an American. You can become an American.

H.K.: You can't if you mean getting rid of your "Jewish past."

I.E.: There's no such thing yet as an American?

H.K.: You see every citizen whatever other label he has, is an American and many a non-citizen can become one culturally, without becoming a citizen. "American" is a common term for a union of the differences, differences which may be as profound and conflicting as the difference between South and North; as the difference between Negro and pinkish yellow, called White, and so on.

I.E.: These "racial" color differences are real differences. The differences between North and South are differences that can be dealt with. If you don't like the South you migrate to the North. You can stop being a Southerner; you can become a Northerner. How do you stop being a Jew?

H.K.: You don't stop being a Jew and you don't stop being a Northerner. You see, you confuse temporal with spatial. You say South and North, and you have in mind the geographical differences. But when you say Southerner, you have in mind a person whose way of life which happens to be in that geographical region. But the way of life can be transferred to other places, like Detroit where there are both White and Black Southern communities, or like New York.

I.E.: Let's assume that when, in your own lifetime, you move from the South to the North you carry the South with you, but your children grow up in the North and they become Northerners . . .

H.K.: If they grow up in my family they will become Northerners as Southerners.

I.E.: All right. Now let's take it a step further. What I'm obviously trying to say is that assimilation is possible in individual cases. It's difficult.

H.K.: Assimilation is possible in all cases, but you have to examine the cases to find out what the word designates.

I.E.: Granted. I'm looking for the rationale, and I know many people are, especially those who separate Jew from Judaist, who feel that in doing so they have removed the rationale for a maintenance of the Jewish ingredient.

H.K.: I'm not sure I understand what you mean by a rationale. But if you mean rationalization of a way of behavior, I regard that as essentially irrelevant. The way of behavior gets rationalized only when it is challenged. So long as it is not challenged it is an ongoing activity.

I.E.: But it is apparently being challenged.

H.K.: Well, everything is challenged; breathing is challenged.

I.E.: Very good. Then young people who have identified themselves with all sorts of groups, Black groups, leftist groups, etc., contend that the Jewish group no longer has any significance. There is no point in belonging to it; in fact, in a certain sense, from the point of view of the way it functions, it almost doesn't exist at all. It is a vestige . . .

H.K.: And what is their way of life? Isn't it highly concentrated in the activity of rejecting whatever Jewishness is a constituent of their personality? They become the Jewish anti-Semites; they become the practitioners of self-hatred; they are assimilated only in the sense that they put on masks and gowns instead of absorbing and reconciling the two cultures. They wage a constant internal warfare which they project externally in the ways you mention and many others. Take, for example, a very interesting instance: you know who are the Chaim Zhitlowsky Foundation.

I.E.: No—I know who Chaim Zhitlowsky was.

H.K.: What do you know about him?

I.E.: About him? A Yiddishist who believed in Diaspora Nationalism; he was a disciple of Dubnow.

H.K.: I have received from the Chaim Zhitlowsky Foundation a while ago the Chaim Zhitlowsky Award. When they came to me to offer the Award I was warned by some of my Yiddishist friends that they were Reds, that the group had been communist, had had the Izvestia attitude, that they had held the position that nationalism is no good, distinctions between people did no good. Their slogan had been, Workers of the world unite, you have nothing to lose but your chains. They had been "patrioten" of the *Freiheit* and still are; they had, of course, rejected Judaism and the Hebrew Scriptures. Which may or may not have been so. But today the Foundation is maintaining a set of Yiddishist schools. Its members call their faith "secular Judaism," themselves "secular Jews." They adapt—especially they adapt the Prophets, but as part of the whole of classical Jewish history, all of the biblical material to current neo-Marxist conceptions, and they have become Zionistic in intent. They are critical of the Russians, etc. Were they assimilated assimilationists? What happened to these people?

I.E.: I think we know what happened.

H.K.: What? I think they came to recognize that they could not, without committing a kind of suicide, without going mad, segregate the past and the future, and that the past had to be the total past. If they at birth had been of Russian or Chinese non-Jewish families, they could not have grown up as Jews. To live a life is to be process of time; it is to be a present in which the future is constantly added to the past. The whole past is not destroyed, but it's transformed. If one is healthy, living is an ongoing internal orchestration of future with past. It is to maintain the well balanced healthy personality, that is labelled "integrated."

I.E.: Let me conclude with one or two questions about the situation in our own country now, and if we have a moment perhaps you might say something about Israel. Do you feel as many of us do that our freedoms are shrinking?

H.K.: Not at all. I think they've expanded. They've expanded immensely since the Second World War. There are always reactions. At present there's Republican-Dixie reaction. But think, for example, what has happened for the people without power, in the attitude of all people. Think to begin with of the mode of expression that started, shall we say with Franklin Roosevelt: "The Four Freedoms," and follow through to the formulations of Lyndon Johnson. You will, I feel sure, find them consistent in idea with the American faith, the religion of America which is tantamount to a religion of religions shared alike by Christians, Judaists, Moslems, Buddhists, Humanists, Atheists. With all their internal divergences and conflicts, they form the Union.

I.E.: You feel equally optimistic about Israel?

H.K.: If you mean in this respect, yes. If Israel survives, the basic assumptions, stated in a utopian way by Theodor Herzl's *Altneuland,* and implemented to some extent by the whole kibbutz movement, from Poale Zion on. . . .

I.E.: You say *if* Israel survives. I'd like to hear a comforting word about the situation as of March 1970.

H.K.: I can't give you comforting words. The image, the impression—more than an impression—I got in the 50's when I made a study, *Utopians at Bay,* has been confirmed by the developments. And Israel is Job holding fast to its integrity against overwhelming force. Israel is confronting what is the equivalent of omnipotence. Israel is without *bona fide* friends—and that is true of all little nations. But especially Israel serves as an instrument of policy for the big powers. Much more so than the Arabs. What Israel has to depend on is the conflict of those powers: for if once they agreed about Israel, Israel would either have to fight for its survival to the last ditch everywhere, or give up its aspiration.

Now the true friend of Israel is not primarily the power holders. It is the enlightened opinion of the free world. Insofar as Israel's internal politics alienates that opinion, the politics are a crippling if not a suicidal act. For this reason alone it were better that the internal minority should act on the recognition that equal liberty of conscience for all Jews, whether or not Judaists, is a *sine qua non* if Israel is to hold and gain *bona fide* friends rather than make the internal compromises which alienate Israel's true friends. Those seem to me a piece of shortsightedness. The unity they pretend to deceives no one, and is strengthened only so long as an enemy presses, but disappears as soon as that enemy is removed. If that enemy were removed, the internal history of Israel would record the process of liberation which is postulated both by the Israeli Declaration of Independence and our own, and by the Universal Declaration of Human Rights to which Israel is a signatory. Liberation will come in the process of give and take, compromise after compromise, but always with a greater expansion of the field of liberty. The Supreme Court decision in the Shalit case is one step forward in the *kulturkampf*, and I would anticipate, other things being equal, that this step will be followed by others, although not in my lifetime . . .

I.E.: What you're suggesting is, I think, by implication, that if the Great Powers don't come to some understanding, then nobody will survive and if they do come to an understanding there is a good chance for Israel.

H.K.: It takes two to make peace; only one to make war. Now Israel would make peace. The enemy won't. His idea of peace is the complete subjugation or destruction of Israel.

I.E.: Yes, there is no doubt about that.

$\boxed{16}$ Toward a Philosophy of Adult Education

I

Everyone, whether he knows it or not, has a philosophy. At the very least, he has the kind of philosophy that the shepherd in Shakespeare's *As You Like It* has. It is the kind of philosophy we all have, a quality of common sense, and is unreflective. We recognize it when the questions are raised; we say, "Why, yes, this is what I wanted to know." But the answers are nonprofessional and for professionals, nonprofessional philosophy can't be truly philosophical. It is couched in language too ordinary and is given forms too common to meet their standards. Similarly, administrators don't like the actualities of housekeeping because the language of the homemaker is not professional and, therefore, somehow, does not bespeak a mystery which can be imparted through schooling.

Now, professional philosophy is a mystery. It possesses an

189

historic vocabulary undergoing continuous modifications by usage. Certain issues, which are functions of the recurrent human predicament and always manifest personal variations, are abstracted from the personal and presented in verbal formulae as the persistent problems of philosophy. What the presentations actually do is utter an ongoing debate, a debate which started when people began to talk philosophically. Convention names Periclean Athens as the place of the great beginning. It developed there from a response to the problems of what we are disposed today to call a "democratic" society. True, in our sense, Periclean Athens was anything but a democratic society. In fact Athenian democracy developed as the avocation of the minority of Athenians who owned slaves and married women to earn their livings for them, and so were free to spend their lives in other ways. One way was to talk out issues of state instead of fighting them out. They soon discovered that opposed interests could thus get to a consensus in which each party benefited more than it could by fighting. They learned that talking issues out has a greater survival function than fighting them out. That is, they learned the value of the democratic process. It is a formation which takes shape as talking together becomes debate, disputation, and develops into inquiry. As the formation emerges, it elaborates. The talkers become aware that their talk has a structure. We call the structure grammar. Soon they see that the grammar has a structure. We call that structure "logic." Logic is a word for certain rules of talking. These rules some sections of Western mankind have modified into what is known as scientific method.

Most of philosophy is logical—i.e., philosophers talk according to certain rules called "laws of thought." They argue creeds and codes and points of view. They shape them into "systems" of philosophy. Each system discloses its own characteristic resolution of the issues being debated. Systems get composed because talking is, among the diverse activities of man, to some degree an independent variable. It began perhaps in the chatter of ancestral apes, and the societies of their unmutated descendants, our cousins, are sometimes described by students as societies of chatter—they make more noise by sounding than by doing. We ourselves make a maximum of noise by sounding as against doing. Man is par excellence the talking animal. Our sounds begin as expression, and develop into communication. When they get the shapes of grammar and logic, they become discourse. All languages, including the mathematical, are first ordered sounds serving as symbols. Such sounds are either concomitants of doing, like the noises we make simply in breathing and, of course, in talking together. But there are many elemental ones. For example—you start burping a baby. The baby hears its own burp and the burp becomes a term in baby language. How this happens has never been adequately studied by the psychologists who have speculated about it. Starting a philosophical discourse from an infant burp can well seem comic. But who can truly tell out of what immediately comic initiation a fruitful discovery can come? Discoveries and inventions figure so much as matters of luck and courage—sometimes more courage than luck, but luck is always a condition.

Now let us pass from germinal burps to systematic philosophies as their history presents them to a would-be professional student, rather than to a potential philosopher. We cannot fail to note that the philosophic systems are many and various. They consist of divergent and often conflicting statements about the universe, about human nature, human fate, and about the good and evil of them for the human beings who are asking the questions to which the systems give answers. The questions are as recurrent as the answers are different. They are questions we can't help asking: *What is it?*—"it" being the entire aggregate of the world around us. *What is it good for?* If "it" is something we like and want to keep, we also want to know how we may do this ["the conservation of values"]; if we don't like and want to rid ourselves of "it," we need to know how to do that ["the problem of evil," the liquidation of sin, etc.]. Each philosophic system offers its own resolution of these vital questions. Since the resolutions differ, a final question follows. Each true believer challenges the others with a demand for proof. Each asks them and himself, *How do you know?*

On the record, replies to this question have assumed certain patterns. For example: you make a statement; I believe you are mistaken, I say *How do you know?* You might retort, "What, you don't believe!" and beat me up, or knock me down. If I keep challenging your statement, you might threaten, "I'll tie you to a stake and burn you alive." Perhaps you retort: "I'll prove it to you by logic"; or, "It has been revealed to me by infallible authority"; or, "So you don't believe me. Well, let's look at this thing I've told you about together, let's examine it as a whole and in its parts. Then we may agree whether my statement has been correct or incorrect."

These different ways of answering the question *How do you know?* are aspects of the philosophic discipline of "epistemology" or theory of knowledge. The current variation of this discipline is called "analysis." In some of its manifestations analysis is a doctrine about "scientific method." It includes an enormous elaboration of symbols and symbols of symbols, which is called "logistics," "mathematical logic" etc., etc.

Answers to the questions: *What is it? What is it good for? How do you know?* build up into the various branches of the philosophic enterprise. *What is it?* is answered by metaphysics, cosmology and theology, severally and jointly. *What is it good for?* is answered by ethics, esthetics, value theory, and the like. *How do you know?* is answered by epistemology, logic, logistics, philosophy of science, and so on. The answers are signalized by some key-word signifying a "school of thought." Even if the data of experience were the same, such philosophies as Materialism and Idealism, in treating of the data, not only differ from each other but diverge from within. There are many different Materialisms, many different Idealisms.

Suppose that you are some variety of Idealist, say a Christian Scientist, then you are altogether certain that matter isn't what it seems. That when you sit on a chair, you sit on mortal error; when you are sick, even to the point of death, your ailment is mortal error. But in order to live on in our culture you have to sit on chairs and deal with illnesses as if they were not errors even though it is of record that the belief that some ailments *are* illusions can contribute to getting rid of them.

Such relations of philosophic constructions to the events of the daily life seem to occur with every system which the history of philosophy records. The reason is, I think, that philosophy concerns itself with all that's not present, all that's absent in the daily life—all the past, all the future—concerns itself with what's usually called "the Beyond" and "the Eternal." These we give a vicarious presence by means of symbols. And our symbols work in our direct experience either to arrest movement and activity or to facilitate them.

Whichever be the case, our symbols serve to help or to hinder our preserving ourselves, our going on living. We postulate them as functions of our will and strivings to keep on and not stop or be stopped. For example, here am I writing this paper. I started, say at five minutes after nine on a cold October morning and I have been writing, with my whole personality committed to the action, during the hour past. Could I have stopped absolutely at any moment within the hour except by dying? The hour I have lived has been an hour of ongoing change; I have grown older altering. Yet to cease altering and stay alive unchanged is exactly what philosophers of the great tradition endeavor to prove we do. Let us consider the stopping places, the terminals of our reality, its unquestioned limits—I say unquestioned and not unquestionable because no limit is ever asserted which somebody mightn't question—that philosophers argue about. Let us consider, say, Aristotle's God, that Unmoved Mover toward whom all existences move in their orders and degrees. He is presented as pure reason, alive, contemplating itself; he is shown as "eternal," that is, he lives on but doesn't change, stays ever one and the same; ultimately, he is inalterable consciousness which is conscious only of itself. By so defining God the philosophic imagination presents us with what can be only a temporal process, that is, with enduring awareness, as the timeless instancy which we call eternity. For all that eternity means or can mean is non-temporal; it is a term by means of which we nullify the sequences of variation of which time positively consists. The experience or insight from which discourse shapes the notion of eternity is the common event that some existences outlive, outlast, other existences. To outlast all others is to become "everlasting." The image of such surpassing survival is "the Eternal": it is the present which is unalterably its own future and contains its own past. At its logical limits, it is dead time.

II

I hope that what I have just set down conveys some notion of the paradoxes which philosophic issues issue in. For I wish now to ask: Can the paradoxes be dispensed with when the philosophic issues are those presented in adult education? When we seek a philosophic issue in a human enterprise, we are seeking "principles" as grounds and goals of our doing whatever it is we happen to be doing. "Principle" signifies the kind of active invariance or invariant activity, activity that is, without alteration which Aristotle designates as Nous Poetikos and to which he gives the name "God." As I see and understand "principle," the notion is nourished, first and last, on the feeling that we would like to live on also when we are dead—with the consequence that most men philosophize in order so to design an image of their universe that it should somehow guarantee their staying alive after they are dead.

Now such a guarantee is an ideal. Fundamentally, the philosophic enterprise undertakes to form an image, to define and draw a picture, of what is beyond experience and imagination, a picture of what is behind the Beyond and beyond the Behind. Its matter and mediums it takes from experience and memory. Its methods come from the human drives of which it is a creation. The philosophic enterprise, as a totality, pictures that which, during anybody's lifetime never becomes a totality but is flow of experience changing as it flows, increasing, diminishing, diversifying. Usually, to philosophize is to translate this flux of diversification into an unaltering self-contained whole, always and everywhere the same. Philosophers create many such compositions, such pictures of the universe. And this bothers us; we don't want them to be as diverse and manifold as in fact they are. So we endeavor to unify; we would like our multiverse to be truly a universe, somehow one and the same. We undertake to prove it such, regardless of how tragically its manyness usually thrusts itself into our experience. Again, we would like our cosmos to be made of stuff that somehow guarantees our living on when we are dead, and we undertake, therefore, en philosophe to prove that we are alive although we are dead, and employ our various religious creeds and codes to prescribe techniques by means of which to guarantee where and how we are going to live when we are dead. We call those places heaven, hell, elysium, tartarus, etc. [the philosophical or theological discipline discoursing of them is called "eschatology" and is a very important department of instruction in philosophic endeavors of theological schools]. We would like to dematerialize the material of experience; if not transvalue it into error or illusion, at least to put it under the psychic stuff— "spirit"—we feel ourselves to be. "Matter" figures as a very repulsive content of experience; we avert from sheer matter. In fact, it is so difficult to prehend, that Aristotle, who set the acceptable fashion, placed it beyond and beneath all actually experienced existences. He called it *hulé* and meant by it an opaque, shapeless mobility that reason cannot think nor the will grasp. He designed existence as a hierarchy of forms informing and containing this *hulé*, stretching between it and the pure form which is God. He presented this hierarchy as an unchanging order of excellence, forever one and the same, to which process and variation are incidental and contingent.

In the Aristotelian cosmos, beings exist on different segregated levels, and the passage from one level or kind into another is impossible. But we recognize that however impossible the passage may be "in principle," it goes on all the time in fact. The impossibility is a philosophical impossibility, and such impossibilities, and possibilities as well, are equally articles of faith, affirmations of some eternalist philosophic creed. Change your creed to what is called "evolution," and you nullify the boundaries between levels of existence. Forms do pass over into one another. We talk of the *origin* of species—i.e., of forms—we labor to think as well as experience reality as flow and process, to apprehend principles and order and God as themselves ongoing changes.

This is a bold and arduous endeavor. But in the long run, even the most materialistic of philosophies continue in some mode monistic, somehow make place for a congruent eternity, universality and spirituality that will serve somehow, somewhere, at some time, to preserve or repeat our personal identity in some form and keep it living on. Confronting the varieties of such cosmic insurance, we choose one or another to use as the symbolic frame of reference for the meaning and value we need to impart to the things we feel and say and do in our day-to-day living. Among conscious philosophers there is a debate over these systems of identification as old as philosophy itself. The debate is the actuality of philosophizing. Its history discloses little consensus or none. At one time one system can become dominant and its alternatives recessive, at another, it is displaced; at all times new variations keep appearing, most of them disappear unnoticed or are forgotten or destroyed. A few struggle on, altering their predecessors as they persist by suffusing them with their own qualities, somewhat in the same way as the meaning of the last word I have written suffuses the meaning of the preceding words. The finished sentence communicates a complete meaning which only this sequential suffusion could create. For this meaning all the words of the sentence have to be read together in the order that I have written them, otherwise the sentence communicates no idea. It is an organization of temporal parts into a temporal whole of the kind that all living manifests, and that today's physics discloses as perception of the ultimate processes of existence.

III

Suppose we call such ultimates quanta. Then the stream of experience may be interpreted as a confluence and diffluence of quanta compounding forever into the manifold varieties of organization and reorganization, which experience learns and the sciences search out. To live on, that is, presently to enlarge one's past and to achieve a future, is somehow to absorb—i.e., to learn —in such wise that the learner is able by means of his philosophic faith to shape the unshaped future as a transformation of his past. In effect, learning is a constant alteration of the past, and this is how and why learning is living and living is learning. We learn at all times, in all places, even when asleep. But the learning we are presently concerned with is that which takes place under special, segregated conditions. It forms a very specific syndrome of ongoing orchestrated changes. "Orchestrated," not "integrated," since to integrate is usually to liquidate a many into a one, to digest diversity into homogeneity, and I don't believe that diversity is ever rendered homogeneous. Actually, we find or effect *unions* not unities; we achieve consensus, not unanimity. I believe that this holds for all relationships, especially among humans. From the particles in the nucleus of an atom and the electrons orbiting round the nucleus, to the United Nations, the relationships are orchestral, the wholes are unions. So long as the unions endure, they do so as the interplay of their members, they do so as orchestrations.

Suppose now we set adult education in the frame of reference of this conception, within the lines of this perspective; then we have brought the philosophic issues into adult education.

What is it?, we ask first. *What shall we look for as the stuff of adult education?* We may decide to look for an abstract essence, for a definition which would signify the same thing always, everywhere and in every way. Or we may accept its diversities as we encounter them and try out ways of bringing them together in such wise that they'll spontaneously stay together. If we can't arrange a peaceful confederation, then we can at least continue talking the alternatives out instead of having to fight them out.

Next we ask, *what is adult education good for?* Do we mean good for ourselves, for others, or for both? If we earn our living by adult education, the answer is to that degree obvious, however we may conventionally meet it by a religious appraisal of our occupation. We justify what we do by invoking an image of society such that it must accept our doings as good and right for this society, as essential to its survival. We invoke its survival as the sanction of our earning our living thus and not otherwise. If actual society rejects the image of our role, if it refuses the sanction, then we reshape it into another image in the light of which we justify our vocation as rebellion or reform; and we define adult education as an engine of social change or social revolution. Or contrariwise, we invoke the state-of-things-as-they-are for the measure of the good and the right, for the sanction of our livelihoods, and use adult education in order to nourish and strengthen the *status-quo.* The record reports the invocation of all these ways of answering: *What is it good for?* Conformity, rebellion, reform, are interrelated and members of one another. It shows them often to be functions of fear and hope, of courage, insight, and luck. Insofar as adult education is a new turn in the overall role of education in the United States, I am disposed to believe that courage is the ultimately determining factor.

That we cannot separate the question *What is Adult Education good for?* from *What does it do?* goes without saying. And it should go without saying that we may not put the latter question without also asking *do to whom? good for whom?* within the configurations of peoples and places we call society. Suppose we consider the learner or educatee—or let us call him the customer, the individual consumer, of adult education. Either it is imposed on him as military training is imposed on army recruits or he desires and seeks it out as he desires and seeks out other goods and services. Suppose he freely becomes a learner, freely assumes the responsibilities of the role which relates him to his educators, and pays them for what they are doing for him even as he pays his doctor, his minister, his lawyer or any other social functionary he employs. Now comes a question *How can the teacher of adults and the adult learner best get together?* The learner is to alter his future by acquiring what is the teachers' past. Are the latter facilitating his learning or are they working to conform his future to their past?

What the answer may be does not primarily depend on the kind of knowledge and knowhow teachers are equipped with. It depends primarily on the kind of persons they are. Personality determines which of the three modes of teacher-pupil relations comes into play—the authoritarian mode, the democratic mode or the conventional mode, which tends toward the authoritarian. Now the schooling syndrome is such that every teacher is an authority to his pupil simply in virtue of his title. Call a person teacher, give him a position behind a desk on a platform, and you have implied that he has superior possession of "the truth." Why? Partly because the pupil believes what he has heard said about the teacher or perhaps because he has read in the teacher's books or because the teacher has a degree and is called doctor or professor or simply teacher; and partly because he sits where he sits and so holds a position of authority analogous to the authority which a police uniform imparts to the common man inside it. The authority lasts only as the future confirms it, and its educational role follows from how it is confirmed. The learner's initial acceptance of teacher-authority is the starting-point in the necessary exercise of the teacher's art and the *how* of the latter is a projection of the teacher's personality. If some authoritarian personality has a sadistic attitude, however disguised, toward his pupils; if in his classroom he is a top-sergeant of the marines, then, regardless of what he may have been taught in teachers' colleges and the like, his sadism will unfailingly fail him as a teacher.

Teacher-pupil relations have also been assimilated to the relation between leaders and followers. Seeing them as such has, I'm afraid, brought out a good many fantasies about leadership and "leadership-training" in education. Fantasies, because as the record discloses, teaching can inform, teaching can help improve the methods of persons who come into positions of leaders, naturally, spontaneously; but cannot make such leaders of persons who are imposed or who impose themselves *ad hoc*. The dynamic differentia is not the scope of instruction, at least so far as my own studies go. Among the variety of teacher-pupil relations we sometimes find forms of teamplay in which the teacher is *primus inter pares*. In such plays teaching and learning figure as cooperative enterprises wherein the role of the teacher is not to instruct but to facilitate the learner's acquiring the knowledge and skill which the teacher already has; to facilitate it in the quickest and most satisfying ways. Generally, teachers depend on how much a learner wants what is offered him, and the common measure of this is the amount of cash he is willing to exchange for it—$50 a point and the like. But there are other, psychologically more critical measures—such as the competing alternatives that he gives up in order to study. Adult education, we have ever to remember, is mostly a night-time activity, always in competition with other modes of spending the leisure hours of the night. The life of the modern urban adult is dual: he lives a day-life and a night-life, and his night-life is shaped by his choice between movies, radio, television, theatre, dancing, sports, cards, "luv" and other modes of "recreation." Education is one more alternative added to these goods between which the adult may choose to spend on by night what he earns by day.

For in our industrial economy the daytime is when a person earns his living, the nighttime is when he lives his life. Living his life is spending what he earns, is freely spending himself. To convince people to spend themselves and to spend their earnings on what we call adult education, and not on competing alternatives, seems to be a paramount task of the adult education movement, and confronts it with a fundamental philosophic issue—the issue of "values."

Today this issue seems to be a critical one for our "democratic" urban communities. The present world-wide strains and tensions have rendered it an issue of vital urgency. We can date its diversified formation from the First World War, and it looks as if the next generation, and the next, are going to experience the state of the world as the brink of disaster. Already our own generation are responding to the needs of managing and using the new sciences, the new machines, and the new instruments of communication, production and destruction, with views and works aiming to alter the patterns of community and the relational orders of men and women and occupations. They are searching and seeking in philosophies old and new for a perspective of existence and value in which to set these innovations. They crave a creed and a code, a design for living with them in equal liberty and equal safety. They are altering the ancestral scale of values that ordained the education of free men. They are reappraising the import of the humanities, which used to be the substance of liberal education, for the survival and growth of a free society of free men. Even more, they are reappraising the import of religion. They are looking with ever greater concern to what is more incommensurably human than religion and the humanities—to what is appraised the most signal differentia is of the human spirit, to the knowledge which is at once both insight and power—to mathematics and the sciences.

The most signal differentia!

The most signal differentia because nothing could be more tangent to the continuities of human life with animal life than mathematics, the sciences and the technics which use them. Although the humanities distinguish us from the rest of the animal world, they do not alienate us from it; on the contrary, they disclose our kinship with it. But mathematics and the sciences do alienate us from it. They rocket us off into the incommensurables of space and time where animals can neither follow nor accompany us. The sciences may demonstrate but cannot express our animal kinships. Biological sciences, which purport to do so, ignore both that which renders mankind different from other animals, and the arts in which both disclose their kinship.

I refer of course to discourse, of which the discourse of reason is the most divergent. I refer to the talk that is intrinsic to the workings of civilization, and especially to the talk we call "science." Its theme is the same as the theme of the humanities, but the consequences of its formulations and handlings of the theme have been an enormous expansion of consciousness, a liberation from ancestral fears, an increase of man's powers over the natural conditions of his existence, and a new fear—the fear of men's use of these powers. On the record, science has been the great liberator. Hence, even though it threatens a new bondage, it may not be disregarded in any design for a liberal education, especially of adults. As I have repeated so often, that is liberal which liberates. Liberation may be achieved by learning, via the methods of science, how to repair a motor car or a gas stove, how to read the Greek tragedians or the theories of Einstein. If learning can also imprison the learner's mind, as it often does, the lock-up is due to the *how*, not to the *what* of learning. I have known both scientists and agonists of the liberal arts who seemed to me imprisoned in their disciplines; imprisoned because they shut out or cut off whatever varied from their knowings and their ways of knowing. They were segregationists of the spirit who excommunicated all the rest of the diversifying world.

A true liberal doesn't, however, excommunicate anything. His spirit is the spirit of science at its optimum, ever curious, ever exploring, experimenting, endeavoring to understand, to discover what a theory is or isn't good for, to communicate what he finds out, and to put it to work for equal liberty and equal safety wherever he can. As he learns, his learnings suffuse his past and render his future different from his past. This is how his education is liberal, and progressively liberating. As I read the record, however, I judge that what has usually been called liberal education has been an endeavor to render the future merely a repetition of the past. Although even mere repetition cannot help bringing some alteration along with it, the alterations are, I would say, fundamentally regressive. Suppose, for example, that a smoker who habitually smokes five cigarettes a day, multiplies his smokes to twenty-five. Certainly tobacco salesmen would call the increase progress, and the smoker might agree with them. Suppose, however, that he sets the increase in relation to the totality of his appetites, to his health, and to the sums he might have saved for bourbon or milk or neckties or paperbacks: would he not then consider himself, perhaps unregretfully, to have regressed? By intensifying his taste for tobacco, by concentrating on his consumption of it, he has lost the power and opportunity to savor and enjoy other goods; he has rendered his economy of life an economy of scarcity, not abundance. True, mankind think the life more abundant in two ways. One is to think it as an amassing of one and the same good. The other is to think it as an orchestration of a diverse multitude of goods. Genuinely liberal education must needs be an orchestration of a diverse multitude of learnings.

For the adult, such an orchestration is the test and measure of a liberal education. Adults come to school with formed habits, with fixed prejudices which serve them as principles, with maybe an intense yet certainly narrow consciousness. They may possess an abundance of some one field of knowing, but such possession is a poverty in that it is maintained by shutting out so much more that can enrich and empower and fulfill them as free men. The adult educator aspires to win them to become seekers of this liberating diversity. Moreover their education, when successful, endows them with satisfactions that but multiply and diversify their spiritual hungers.

Which, among the satisfactions, is the essential one? Is it "vocation"? Is it "culture"? The distinctions we make between these two, together with all the other traditional distinctions, are issues of an ongoing debate among philosophers of education. The disputants argue over content rather than consequence, diet rather than nourishment. Now as I see the typical adult, his vital need is liberation. With respect to satisfying this need, consider a moment two contrasted doctrines of what has been recently preached as "the national purpose," but is in education "the national goal." How, I ask, have we imagined the Jones we want Homo Americanus to keep up with whether as "purpose" or as "goal"? What ideal image of the American do we desire Americans to embody? One answer was recently provided us by James Truslow Adams. He gives it in the phrase, *The American Dream.* The other was provided us by Theodore Parker more than one hundred years ago. Interpreting our Declaration of Independence, he gives it as *The American Idea.*

I think that those of us who believe in adult education as essential to the national being are up against the issue of the relationship of Dream and Idea, of abundance and freedom, and of the primacy of freedom.

For as Americans we by and large believe that our society is a free society postulated on the principles of the Declaration of Independence and more or less successfully implemented by means of the Constitution, and perhaps more retarded than facilitated by the houses of Congress and the presidency. The nation's history is the record of unyielding struggles to keep embodying the Idea of Freedom in the American way of life, to make of the way what I have elsewhere called a discipline of freedom. The discipline of freedom is a form of "togetherness" such as the art of disputation evinces—good manners in discourse. It builds on the recognition by each one of the right of the others to be different, and of the different to work out and fulfill themselves in their differences equally with one's self. It builds on the steady purpose to find out how, in any endeavor of the mind, the hand or the heart or of all three jointly, people who are different from each other can act together with each other, and each fulfill his selfhood more abundantly than he could by going it alone.

And this discipline builds on the recognition by each that, as learner, he begins and ends in aloneness. For learning is like eating; nobody can do it for anybody else; no cook, no matter how good, can guarantee that the feeder will be nourished and will make a good digestion of the dishes the cook has prepared. Let us agree, for this argument at least, that there is an analogy between cooks and teachers; then it would follow that the teacher's moment of truth comes in arousing and nourishing such a hunger for the food of the soul that the eater will go on eating of his own motion and not depend on the initiating conditions and subsequent stimulation of the classroom. Of course, children do learn to like spinach, and as Kurt Lewin demonstrated in a number of dietary experiments during the Second World War, they got to dislike spinach only from the contagion of their elders' attitudes. Spontaneously, spinach had an equal chance to be tasted, chewed and swallowed, and often was. Those who watch what an infant puts in its mouth note that infant curiosity is not limited to any object or field. We must needs take the recovery of curiosity, its discipline and upkeep, to be a goal intrinsic to adult education. I believe this recovery to be a fundamental task which many theories of learning simply fail to confront.

A final word now about the anxieties of teachers of adults. I have myself been an adult educator nearly fifty years. I became one because, during World War I, I was associated with people deeply aware that a cleavage had opened up in our culture; they foresaw a future which appears, unhappily, to verify their prevision completely. They believed and hoped that extending education to adults might help avert the hazards they anticipated. John Dewey's *Democracy and Education*, please recall, was published in 1916. Its theme was the education of children and youth. Its background was a certain amount of experimentation and development. In the national life, the design for education was to expand and improve elementary and secondary schooling wherever practicable in the nation's aggregation of educational systems. Concurrently, a certain concern became evident regarding the deficiencies of the colleges and universities. There were discussions, especially among scholars mobilized for war work and men of affairs and of letters anxious about the impact of the War on the American Idea. Many of the scholars were university professors who, because Woodrow Wilson was himself an ex-professor, had been variously mobilized for the national defense. It was about then that the expression "brain trust" came into use and the idea of "egghead" was being laid. The notion that intellectuals could exercise a vital function in public affairs—a notion traditionally deprecated and scorned—began to receive acceptance. Intellectuals like Thorstein Veblen, Wesley Clair Mitchell, like Walter Lippman and other members of Col. House's *Inquiry*, who were busy in Washington and elsewhere with wartime economic policy, military strategy, terms of peace and of its organization, became dismayed by the inadequacies of college-educated citizens to meet with wisdom and skill the issues of the national being, of the national defense and of their international import. Out of their dismay came a divergent conception of adult education. Its expression and interpretation was concurrent with the widespread movement to expand and improve the nation's school systems. The effective effort was concentrated on elementary and secondary schooling. Although "higher education" is now receiving anxious attention, emphasis continues to be laid, not wrongly, on the "lower." It was the depression of the '30s which brought what is now called "continuing education" toward the foreground of communal concern. That, I believe, became important incidentally, through the operations of the WPA. It heightened the consciousness of *whys* and *wherefores* of adult education. It challenged its identification with the "Americanization" of immigrants and with "university extension." Mostly, the consciousness was the professionals'. First a function of the process of providing employment for disemployed teachers, it spread to other citizens concerned about the adult psyche, and about its health and its responsibilities, personal and public. The adult education it envisioned and argued for was quite different from "university extension," and from the self-education of the Women's Clubs (this was a true adult education endeavor, a phase of the self-liberation of American women). Women's clubs are now recessive. Their urgency seems to have spent itself at last, when women won the vote by the constitutional amendment which was one more step toward the realization of the American Idea, a step in our country's ongoing struggle toward the parity of the different in rights and liberties. In many ways women's clubs are now as tangent to the realities of this struggle as the Daughters of the American Revolution. Other interests absorb our women everywhere, except maybe in the South. Thus, the League of Women

Voters is a women's design for the adult education of both women and men in the issues confronting the Republic. The methods it employs could reward the study of any group concerned with educating adults.

The next generation of both sexes will, I believe, find themselves seeking "continuing education," seeking higher education, as adults, on the same scale as now we seek to educate the unadult. They will do so, whatever they may mean by "adult." This term is to me strictly a cultural symbol, with meanings that vary from culture to culture, and from region to region within any culture. A human adult is not the same as a physiologically adult animal. In many ways an individual's adulthood is determined rather by the mores of the community he grows up in than by anything in his somatic condition. "Adult" is a social-cultural variable, not a psychosomatic constant, and the adult's education must come to grips with the challenges this presents.

As compared with the educators in the schools and colleges, the adult educator is the pioneer of a movement which can fail only if it is abandoned. Instituting it, developing it into an organic component of the nation's educational establishment involves many struggles, with many defeats. But struggle and defeat are incident to all victorious wars. Winning the war for adult education needs above all the courage to fight it, to bet lives and fortunes and sacred honor on an outcome that cannot be a sure thing. Opposed by education's cultural alternatives, by academic and other vested interests, adult education may or may not overcome them by means of the findings of inquiries or researches. More vital to victory are the choices and the decisions such findings prompt. Those are issues of the personal life. Whatever one finds out, whatever one rejects, may be to a different individual as significant a value to bet on as that which one accepts. The readiness to take the risks of decision is nuclear to all free enterprise, and nuclear above all to the free enterprise of the mind, its sine qua non. Deciding is betting. It is betting that some aspect of the past which one creates by learning can help determine the undetermined future in such a way that the determination will enrich, enhance and transform our lives as we live on, and grow up and grow older. The transformation of the self, which is the all of successful learning, keeps on so long as life is lived. At any age, education is presumed to provide conditions that favor its optimal, if not supreme facilitation, and it is no less essential to adulthood than to youth.

ACKNOWLEDGMENTS

My thanks to the following journals and magazines in which chapters of this book appeared as articles and essays: *Educational Theory, Emory University Quarterly, The Hourglass, Journal of Educational Sociology, Journal of Philosophy, Journal of Public Law, Journal for the Scientific Study of Religion, New York Law Forum, Reconstructionist, Saturday Review, The Standard;* and to the following publishers of books in which chapters appeared: The John Day Company, Inc. (from *Sidney Hook and the Contemporary World,* edited by Paul Kurtz, copyright © 1968 by The John Day Company, Inc.), Harper & Row, Publishers, Inc. (from *This Is My Faith,* edited by Stewart G. Cole, copyright © 1956 by Stewart G. Cole), and UNESCO (from *Democracy in a World of Tensions,* edited by Richard McKeon with the assistance of Stein Rokkan).

59262

AC   Kallen, Horace.
8   What I believe
.K312   and why--maybe.

DATE DUE

GAYLORD   PRINTED IN U.S.A.